100

THINGS TO DO IN

ALBANY

BEFORE YOU

DIE

SANDRA FOYT

REEDY PRESS

100

THINGS TO DO IN

ALBANY

BEFORE YOU

DIE

Lark Street

CONTENTS

Sports and Recreation

• •

Culture and History

• •

Shopping and Fashion

• •

ACKNOWLEDGMENTS

This book would not have been possible without the friends and followers who have shared their favorite places in and around Albany and continue to inspire me daily.

Many of you began the journey with me on the family travel blog *Albany Kid*, following me onto the empty-nest project, *Getaway Mavens*. And then, when I returned my focus home, you helped support and promote *Albany Traveler*.

Meeting you online and sometimes in person has been a privilege. You've helped me raise my children and find the most delicious ice cream in New York. Thank you so much!

And a heartfelt thank-you to the partner who is always up for an adventure and our two "Albany kids" who inspired me to search for things to do in Upstate New York.

I'm deeply grateful for our never-ending travels.

PREFACE

Twenty-five years ago, I arrived in Albany, New York, in a Toyota 4Runner overstuffed with a toddler, two retrievers, and a partner who had happily joined me on a two-month road trip across the US and Canada. We moved into a rental and, a year later, my youngest was born on the day we closed on a house in the woods.

It wasn't until a few years later that I set out to get to know Albany. I then launched a family travel blog and went all out to chronicle every nook and cranny of what locals affectionately refer to as "Smallbany."

Once the home of the Mohican and Mohawk people, the Dutch sent Henry Hudson to explore the area in 1609, eventually establishing the city of Albany in 1686. There are many historical tales to be told here.

And yet Albany, the second-oldest city in the country, balances history with innovation. Now at the forefront of the Tech Valley's nanotechnology industry, major microchip manufacturers built cutting-edge factories here, bringing new jobs and opportunities.

Since I moved in, the MVP Arena—christened the Knickerbocker Arena in 1990 by its first performer, Frank Sinatra—has changed its name twice more, first from the Pepsi Arena and then from Times Union Center. The list of outstanding restaurants has grown well beyond the confines of this book, and we finally have a Whole Foods, Trader Joe's, and possibly a Costco before year's end.

Despite these changes, Albany is still Smallbany in all the best ways.

• •

Live here long enough, and you recognize friends at bars and restaurants, even when you include venues throughout the Capital District. And because the Capital Region encompasses seven counties, a dozen state parks, and countless lakes, creeks, and "kills" (the Dutch word for water channel), you're never far from green space.

Perched on the shore of the Hudson River along the eastern edge of Upstate New York, a 45-minute drive from Massachusetts or Vermont, Albany is surrounded by forested mountains. From here, it's an easy day trip to hike and photograph the Adirondack, Appalachian, Catskill, Green, or Berkshire Mountains.

I've come to appreciate the rolling hills of farmland punctuated by dramatic vistas of cascading waterfalls and the colorful splendor of fall foliage season. This is New York, with the rich heritage and diverse stories of its people, surrounded by a treasured land that doesn't change at all.

Since I launched *Albany Kid* in 2010, I've gone on to freelance with other publications while developing a travel photography portfolio. I've partnered on a website about romantic getaways and even started another travel blog, *Albany Traveler*, to build on what is here. I've learned that the more I see of Albany and its surroundings, the longer my bucket list grows.

Ready to get started? Check the back of the book for Suggested Itineraries and Activities by Season. Got questions? Join me and other readers on the *Albany Traveler* Facebook page, where we plan tours, photo walks, and other events to share everything we prize about this historic city surrounded by nature.

• •

Cider donuts

FOOD
AND DRINK

DEVOUR
AN OVERSIZED FISH FRY

Ready your appetite for Albany's unique spin on the classic fish fry. This dish dares to go big, featuring a colossal spear of batter-crisped cod or haddock that dramatically overshadows its bun. But it's not just the size that stands out. Here, traditional tartar sauce takes a back seat to a hearty ladle of robust chili sauce, adding a nice heat to the crispy fish. This fish fry is not just about filling up; it's a nod to the area's distinct culinary style that's a bit different from the norm. Pair a sandwich with an award-winning ale at Chatham Brewing, with a thick milkshake at summers-only Gene's Fish Fry, or order the whole fried smorgasbord at Ted's Fish Fry. The original, with multiple locations, has served the region for over 70 years.

Chatham Brewing
59 Main St., Chatham, 518-697-0059
chathambrewing.com

Gene's Fish Fry
300 Troy Rd., Rensselaer, 518-286-3767
facebook.com/people/genes-fish-fry/100063573639596

Ted's Fish Fry
1186 Western Ave., 518-650-8679
203 Wolf Rd., 518-454-9490
tedsfishfry.com

CHARM YOUR SWEETHEART
AT THE IRON GATE CAFE

To know the Iron Gate Cafe is to love the Iron Gate Cafe. Capital Region residents so cherish the eatery that it is consistently rated "most loved by locals" on the neighborhood network app Nextdoor. Conveniently located in historic Center Square near Washington Square Park, the café makes good use of a refurbished 19th-century mansion. Cozy rooms and a cheerful courtyard garden setting elevate the popular brunch spot to an ideal date venue. Focusing on breakfast and lunch, with breakfast served all day, the menu offers a variety of Benedicts, while the raspberry brie french toast is a particular favorite. There's something for everyone, from sandwiches and wraps to salads and vegan options, perfectly paired with brunch cocktails or coffee. Whether you're looking for a quick bite or a languid brunch with loved ones, Iron Gate Cafe is an enticing locale that transforms food and historic ambiance into an unforgettable experience.

182A Washington Ave., 518-445-3555
irongatecafe.com

TRY A REGIONAL SPECIALTY: THE MINI HOT DOG
AT GUS'S

In and around Albany, there is a delectably unique take on what we think of as hot dogs. Forget the standard six-inch frank you might find elsewhere; here, it's all about the four-inch-long mini, snugly settled in a similarly sized bun. But it's the toppings that genuinely define this regional specialty. Albany-area mini dogs are slathered with bright yellow mustard, generously sprinkled with chopped onions, and crowned with a tantalizing chili-like meat sauce that varies from place to place in taste and consistency. Gus's Hot Dogs—an unassuming roadside stand—is said to have the tastiest meat sauce in the area. The menu here is simple but filling; in addition to the mini dogs, Gus's offers its equally famous Greek burgers or sausage sandwiches.

212 25th St., Watervliet, 518-273-8743
gusshotdogswatervliet.com

CHOW DOWN ON CLASSIC COMFORTS
AT CAPITAL CITY DINER

You can order a stack of buttermilk pancakes any time of day, every day, at the family-run Capital City Diner. Breakfast when you like it is just one reason this retro 1950s-style diner tops the Capital Region's "Best Of" lists year after year. With its gleaming chrome decor, comfy booths, and friendly service, this old-school diner transports you to a bygone era where comfort dishes reign supreme. Find five kinds of Italian parmigianas alongside Greek favorites like gyro and souvlaki, juicy burgers, hearty sandwiches, and homemade pies. Add a varied selection of cocktails to the usual beer and wine, and for late-night snacks, consider the calamari or disco fries. Whether you're craving nostalgia or seeking an authentic diner experience, Capital City Diner's broad menu and inviting atmosphere deliver.

1709 Western Ave., 518-250-4261
pilarinoshospitalitygroup.com/capital-city-diner.html

DINE WITH GHOSTS
AT THE OLDE ENGLISH PUB & PANTRY

Travel back to the 1730s with a visit to The Olde English Pub & Pantry, a snug spot in the historic Quackenbush House. Savor the taste of traditional British fare while soaking up tales from the house's eerie past. Built by the industrious Pieter Quackenbush near the clay-rich Hudson River, it's believed that the house's bricks may have come from his own brickyard. As you toss back a pint of Boddingtons Pub Ale, look out for the loaves of bread that reportedly take flight from the shelves, a hint of the house's spectral residents. Whether you come for the food, the history, or the ghostly tales, this haunt offers an unforgettable blend of top-notch hospitality, mouthwatering cuisine, and an intriguing brush with the paranormal.

683 Broadway, 518-434-6533
theoldeenglish.com

TIP

The Olde English Pub & Pantry is located at Quackenbush Square, in the oldest part of Downtown Albany. This is an excellent spot for beginning a visit to the Capital Region. There's plenty of metered parking, and in addition to the restaurant, you'll find the Albany Visitors Center, the Irish American Museum, and the Albany Pump Station.

SATISFY YOUR SWEET TOOTH
AT CIDER BELLY DOUGHNUTS

In the city where Dutch settlers first introduced "Olykoeks" or "oily cakes" (the precursors of modern doughnuts) to the New Netherlands, Cider Belly Doughnuts continues this age-old tradition with a creative twist. The star attraction is the Sugar Daddy, a classic cider donut, which flies off the shelves with hundreds sold each day. Come early; they sell out by late morning. And that's far from all, as their recipe databank holds over 500 inventive offerings, with at least six surprises each week offering treats like the Cereal Killer, Straw BuBBly, or Key Lime Pie. For a tantalizingly grown-up treat, try their booze-infused flavors, crafted in partnership with local distilleries. The Mango Boozy Bellies spiked with Ghost Pepper Tequila or the Tipsy Moose with whiskey from the Albany Distilling Co. are recent crowd-pleasers.

53 Fuller Rd., 518-253-4640
facebook.com/ciderbellydoughnuts

EAT, DRINK, AND PICK YOUR OWN FRUIT
AT INDIAN LADDER FARMS

Almost nothing tastes as sweet as sun-warmed blueberries picked fresh off the bush, except, perhaps, a freshly harvested Honeycrisp apple. Indian Ladder Farms, established in 1916 by Peter G. Ten Eyck, a descendant of some of Albany's early Dutch settlers, offers just that experience. Wander through lush orchards and select the finest fruits to fill your basket. As lunchtime rolls around, grab a spot at the seasonal Yellow Rock Cafe, serving up delectable farm-to-table eats. Then, saunter over to the Indian Ladder Farm Cidery and Brewery. Here, you can sample various beverages crafted on-site in the tasting room or the friendly biergarten. Summer through fall, bring your four-legged friend along on Wednesday nights for food and drink specials just for you and your buddy. Lastly, take advantage of the Farm Market, combining local produce and home-grown artisanal creations.

342 Altamont Rd., Altamont, 518-765-2956
indianladderfarms.com

TIP

Time your visit to arrive during the annual Farming Man Fest held in the summer for a celebration of live music and craft beverages, connecting entrepreneurs and connoisseurs. Ten years in the making, the event draws over 30 breweries plus three distilleries from all around New York.

farmingmanfest.com

PERK UP
AT UNCOMMON GROUNDS

Artisanal coffee and the visual treat of an ever-changing art gallery welcome you at Uncommon Grounds. Freshly roasted coffee beans, processed in-house at the University Plaza location every couple of days, take you on an olfactory trip around the world. And, in case you're wondering, detailed labels identify the region and sometimes the specific farms where the beans were harvested. Non-coffee-drinkers can choose from a wide selection of loose-leaf teas—from sweet and spicy to earthy and everything in between. Complement your order with a freshly baked, hand-rolled bagel lavished with homemade cream cheese or hearty sandwich fillings. It doesn't get more New York than this! The ambiance oscillates between cozy and stimulating, making it a go-to for contemplative afternoons, casual meetups, or the daily caffeine fix.

1235 Western Ave., #5, 518-453-5649
Stuyvesant Plaza, 1475 Western Ave., 518-451-9974
9 Clifton Country Rd., Clifton Park, 518-280-2404
402 Broadway, Saratoga Springs, 518-581-0656
uncommongrounds.com

MORE GREAT COFFEE SHOPS AROUND ALBANY

The Daily Grind, opened in 1976, was the first in the Northeast to roast coffee in-house.
204 Lark St., Ste. 1, 518-427-0464
dailygrind.com

Professor Java's Coffee Sanctuary is just that, multiple rooms providing convivial meeting spaces.
145 Wolf Rd., 518-435-0843
professorjavas.us

Jacob Alejandro, coffee artisan and 2022 US Cold Brew Champion, serves up some of the most inventive lattes.
274 River St., Troy
466 Madison Ave.
jacobalejandro.com

Stacks Espresso Bar offers high-caffeine espressos as well as a full complement of sandwiches, salads, and desserts at several area locations.
488 Broadway, 518-915-1000
260 Lark St., 518-650-6527
652 Albany Shaker Rd., 518-245-6869
stacksespresso.com

TASTE THE FUSION OF FLAVOR AND HISTORY
AT TANPOPO RAMEN

Check out a piece of Albany's history at Tanpopo Ramen. Once known as the Miss Albany Diner and Lil's Diner, this landmark building has a rich past. Constructed in 1941, the diner was listed on the US National Register of Historic Places in 2000. Notably, it served as a set for the 1987 film *Ironweed*, starring Jack Nicholson and Meryl Streep. With its interior of cherry wood, porcelain enameled steel, and geometrically tiled floor, this Silk City Diner model stands as one of the few pre–World War II diners in near-original condition. Today, as Tanpopo, it presents a delicious blend of history and Japanese cuisine. The ramen here is crafted with meticulous attention to authenticity, and a choice of local brews and ciders rounds out the sake selection.

893 Broadway, 518-451-9868
tanpopoalbany.com

RAISE A GLASS
TO A HISTORIC BREW
AT ALBANY ALE & OYSTER

When the Dutch arrived in the early 1600s, the Hudson River Estuary teemed with oyster beds. In the 1800s, New York was the largest supplier of oysters worldwide, and the bivalve was served on street corners and in the fanciest restaurants. By the 1860s, the city boasted 30 breweries, fueling the production and export of the popular Albany Ale, a mild pale ale. That tradition and the city's brewing heritage are fondly recalled at Albany Ale & Oyster. The daily board showcases a good selection of fresh raw oysters, available on the half shell, in addition to a roasted oyster dish and a variety of seafood selections. And although the historic Albany Ale is no longer available anywhere, the bar boasts an impressive array of local brews. Twenty rotating taps promise a new taste with every visit. Expert staff guides you through the ever-evolving beer menu, ensuring the perfect match for your palate.

281 New Scotland Ave., 518-487-4152
albanyaleandoyster.com

TIP
Time your visit for Happy Hour, 3 p.m.–5 p.m., for $2 oysters and $15 lobster rolls.

FEAST ON AUTHENTIC ITALIAN FARE
AT CAFE CAPRICCIO

Treat yourself to a feast at Cafe Capriccio, an Italian restaurant that consistently tops the list of Albany's finest. Known for its dedication to quality, the menu shines with locally sourced meats and vegetables, complemented by mouthwatering homemade desserts. Its cuisine changes with the seasons, maintaining freshness and offering patrons a chance to explore Italy's diverse culinary landscape throughout the year. Book the Chef's Table for an exceptional occasion, available for groups of 10 to 16 guests. Dine family style, sharing plates and stories, hosted by Chefs Jim Rua and Michael Preusser. Jim Rua has multiple cookbooks on Italian cooking to his credit; he's known for a simplicity "that relies more on ingredients than on the manipulation of ingredients." What's more, Cafe Capriccio goes the extra mile by organizing trips to Italy, which allow guests to explore the diverse flavors of the Tuscan countryside firsthand.

49 Grand St., 518-465-0439
cafecapriccio.com

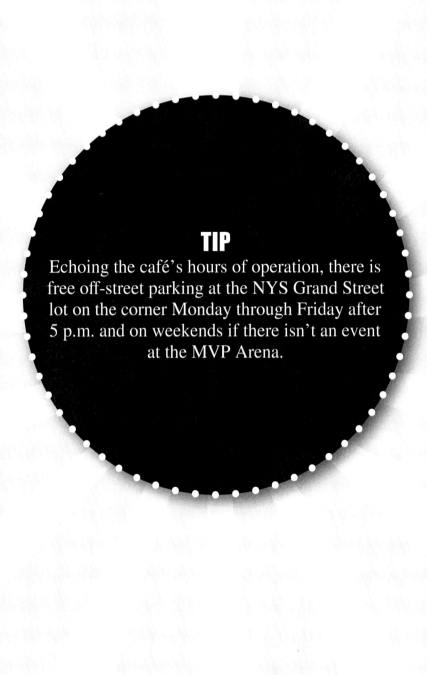

TIP

Echoing the café's hours of operation, there is free off-street parking at the NYS Grand Street lot on the corner Monday through Friday after 5 p.m. and on weekends if there isn't an event at the MVP Arena.

TOAST TO SUSTAINABILITY
AT THE ALBANY PUMP STATION

Common Roots Brewing at the Albany Pump Station stands as a symbol of brewing tradition and innovation. Under the careful stewardship of the father-son team Bert and Christian Weber, this establishment melded the legacy of C.H. Evans Brewing with the fresh vision of Common Roots. Guests enjoy its popular Good Fortune beer, a favorite from Common Roots's lineup, alongside a dynamic selection of two or three new beers released monthly. Each brew is crafted with passion and creativity, blending old-world and contemporary flavors. The menu further exemplifies this ethos with an emphasis on sustainable sourcing. Drawing from local farms, culinary offerings feature farm-fresh beef and vegetables. From farm to table, each dish is a testament to community connection and environmental stewardship. The merger of these two brewing icons has created a destination that not only honors the rich history of the Pump Station but also brings forth a new era in craft brewing and community programming.

19 Quackenbush Sq., 518-409-8248
commonrootsbrewing.com

SIP YOUR WAY THROUGH THE CAPITAL CRAFT BEVERAGE TRAIL

Crafted experiences await those keen to enter the world of hops, grapes, and grains. The Capital Craft Beverage Trail introduces you to passionate artisans dedicated to the craft of brewing, distilling, and fermenting. Traverse this trail, and you'll rub elbows with local brewers, vintners, and distillers eager to share the stories behind every bottle. Pick up a new passport each year to collect stamps from more than 60 member businesses throughout the Capital Region and redeem them for prizes. Remember to check the website for upcoming events!

capitalcraftbeveragetrail.com

SAMPLE ARTISANAL CIDERS
AT NINE PIN CIDER WORKS

New York's pioneering farm cidery, Nine Pin Cider Works, transforms apple varieties harvested from the Capital Region and Hudson Valley orchards into crisp, refreshing brews. Their creative lineup ranges from traditional favorites to unique blends infused with fruits, herbs, and spices. This dedication birthed the Harvest Series—a tribute not only to New York's agriculture but also to its local businesses. Standout creations from this series include the Aurora Blueberry and Montgomery Cherry ciders. One harmonizes beautifully with apples in the co-fermentation process, while the other brings a sour twist. While you can find these ciders at many local bars and restaurants, the taproom offers a perfect opportunity to taste your way through all their offerings, accompanied by a substantial pub menu—featuring a rotating lineup of sourdough pizza as well as hand pies or empanadas sourced from local vendors. Plus, the taproom hosts many fun weekly events from Monday Date Night to Sunday Brunch as well as one-off crafting workshops and occasional Singles Nights.

Check the website's events schedule for monthly production tours. Led by an expert, it's a deep dive into the cider-making process, including cider tastings and a take-home souvenir glass.

929 Broadway, 518-449-9999
ninepincider.com

WAREHOUSE DISTRICT BAR CRAWL

Nine Pin Cider Works is one of several businesses on Broadway in Albany's revitalized Warehouse District. Look for the giant *Nipper* statue on one end (see #63) and the following bars and restaurants:

Lionheart on the Green
952 Broadway, 518-818-0921
albanylionheartpub.com

Lost & Found Bar & Kitchen
942 Broadway, 518-694-0670
lostandfoundalbany.com

Wolff's Biergarten
895 Broadway, 518-427-2461
wolffsbiergarten.com

Fidens Brewing Company Taproom
897 Broadway, 518-608-0014
fidensbrewing.com

Tanpopo Ramen
893 Broadway, 518-451-9868
tanpopoalbany.com

TAP INTO THE REVELRY
AT CITY BEER HALL

City Beer Hall is a lively gastropub housed in a historic telephone company building in the city's heart. With its inventive menus, City Beer Hall transforms locally sourced and seasonal ingredients into dazzling, from-scratch dishes. The joy of this vibrant spot is amplified by its generous offerings: each beer or cocktail purchase is served with a free personal pizza, turning every visit into a celebration. Choose between indoor and outdoor seating for dinner, brunch, or a late-night escapade, and explore beers from the 20 rotating taps featuring the finest craft beverages from the area. The majestic Main Hall—with its grand fireplace, wagon wheel chandelier, and long picnic tables—somehow serves both intimate dates and cheerful happy hour gatherings. City Beer Hall keeps the excitement rolling with tap takeovers, trivia nights, beer pairing dinners, live music, and more, all contributing to an undeniably exuberant atmosphere.

42 Howard St., 518-449-2337
thecitybeerhall.com

TREAT YOURSELF TO DESSERT FIRST
AT CHEESECAKE MACHISMO

Cheesecake Machismo will make you a believer in having dessert first. The quirky, laid-back dessert spot offers a daily rotation of unique cheesecakes from a menu of over 700 flavors. Famed for their innovative and creative concoctions, their menu surprises with quirky combinations such as Lemon Lavender or Maple Bacon. Each slice is a work of art, both visually stunning and tastebud-tantalizing. With a cozy, colorful atmosphere decorated with action-hero collectibles and Capital City Coffee on tap, this shop has an appeal beyond its dessert offerings. Consider taking home a Frankencake, their sampler of multiple flavors for the indecisive dessert lover. Available flavors are posted daily on their Facebook page, but when they sell out, that's it; the shop closes.

293 Hamilton St., 518-427-7019
cheesecakemachismo.com

CELEBRATE GOOD TIMES
AT MCGEARY'S IRISH PUB

Find yourself transported to Ireland when you step into McGeary's Irish Pub. Its warm, welcoming atmosphere and spirited social scene make it the perfect spot for anyone seeking hearty food, heartier drinks, and lively entertainment. Celebrated for its friendly staff and genuine pub ambiance, McGeary's offers an inviting experience. No visit is complete without sampling their authentic Irish cuisine—think comforting shepherd's pie and a perfectly served pint of Guinness. Make sure to join their trivia nights or enjoy a game on the big screen for added fun. The live music, featuring a medley of local talent across diverse genres, adds to the appeal and vivacity of this beloved pub. McGeary's Irish Pub is more than just a dining destination; it's a place to make memories and friends, and more importantly, to toast to good times.

4 Clinton Sq., 518-463-1455
mcgearyspub.com

TIP

As a young boy, *Moby-Dick* author Herman Melville attended the Albany Academies and lived at 3 Clinton Square, the pink house next door to McGeary's Irish Pub.

SNAG A SLICE
AT KAY'S PIZZA

Nothing screams summer like a trip to Kay's Pizza. Perched along Burden Lake, this seasonal restaurant has been dishing up tasty pizzas since 1958. Tables draped in red checkered vinyl tablecloths; a glossy wooden bar lined with tattered, signed dollar bills; and an ancient coin-operated kiddie ride by the entrance all exude a retro vibe. You are likely to find cars overflowing from the parking lot and lining the dirt road, with patrons eagerly waiting on the front porch for a taste of the famous pizza. Expect all the usual flavors and then some unusually delicious combos, such as the Thai chili chicken or Capt. Bill Clam Steam. Apart from that, there's a wide assortment of pub fare and Italian dinners—including the regional favorite, mozzarella sticks with tangy, raspberry-based Melba sauce dip. Top it off with a pitcher of beer, then stop at nearby Moxie's for an ice cream cone for a total dose of nostalgia.

10 Walsh Ln., Averill Park, 518-674-5413
kayspizza.com

SPLURGE AT YONO'S
FOR A BIG NIGHT OUT

Indulgence meets sophistication at Yono's, a gem celebrated not only for its blend of contemporary American cuisine with Indonesian spices but also for an award-winning wine list boasting about 800 labels. Recognized by *Wine Spectator* magazine for over 20 years, Yono's wine selection is an oenophile's dream, expertly curated to enhance every dish. Most recently, the current owner, Dominick Purnomo, was nominated for a Sommelier of the Year award by *Wine Enthusiast*, a testament to his mastery and dedication. Yono's intimate ambiance, and a tasting menu featuring complex dishes such as the 24-Hour Braised Beef Rendang, provide a perfect setting for romance or special celebrations. Dining here isn't just a meal; it's an immersive experience in culinary excellence and wine artistry. As one of the #opentable Top 100 restaurants in the US, a splurge at Yono's is a must for foodies.

25 Chapel St., 518-436-7747
yonos.com

TIP

Whether you're celebrating a special occasion or just looking to treat yourselves, Albany's upscale dining scene won't disappoint. Besides the four-star Yono's, there's also 677 Prime. With its own impressive wine list, this steak house is the perfect setting for an indulgent evening.

677 Broadway, 518-427-7463
677prime.com

INDULGE IN SPIRITED ICE CREAM
AT BOOZY MOO!

Grown-up dessert fantasies come true at Boozy Moo!, where ice cream gets a spirited twist. Combining rich, creamy ice cream with a splash of alcohol, Boozy Moo! offers a selection of flavors that are as delicious to the taste buds as they are inventive. From bourbon-spiked vanilla to tequila-infused strawberry, each scoop is a playful affair. Boozy Moo! is the COVID brainchild of Leyla Kiosse, owner of The Yard: Hatchet House & Bar, an axe-throwing game venue. It also offers imaginative cocktails and a snack menu with charcuterie boards and Dough Bombs. Nonalcoholic options are available, too, ensuring that everyone can partake in the fun. Whether you're toasting a special occasion or embracing the pleasure of a well-crafted treat, Boozy Moo! invites you to celebrate the extraordinary in every spoonful. It's an experience that blurs the lines between traditional dessert and cheerful celebration.

16 Sheridan Ave., 518-631-4002
boozymoo.com
theyardalbany.com

MORE GREAT ICE CREAM

Since 1969, **Moxie's Ice Cream** has been crafting rich, homemade ice cream with flavors ranging from the signature Blue Moon and the round-the-world Vanilla Sampler to mystery flavors like Sweet Corn. Visit often, because once a flavor runs out, it might not return.
1344 Spring Ave., Wynantskill, 518-283-4901
facebook.com/moxiesicecream

Celebrating its 70th season, the **Snowman** serves hard and soft ice cream, sundaes and flurries, shakes and ice cream pies.
531 5th Ave., Troy, 518-233-1714
thesnowmanicecream.com

Sometimes the best ice cream is the one that's convenient. With multiple convenient store locations around the Capital Region, **Stewart's Shops** are a favorite stop for a celebratory cone or a gallon to bring home.
542 Central Ave., 518-482-9671
stewartsshops.com

MANGIA
IN SCHENECTADY'S LITTLE ITALY

Dive into the flavors and traditions of the Mediterranean in Schenectady's Little Italy. This lively neighborhood enclave offers an authentic taste of Italian culture and cuisine in the heart of upstate New York. Your first stop should be More Perreca's, a family-owned restaurant celebrated for its robust Italian American dishes such as lasagna or chicken Parm. It is adjacent to Perreca's Bakery, which has been serving up crusty bread since 1914. Cornells is also a notable find: a community favorite for its classic Italian dishes—the fried calamari is a must—and warm ambiance. Round off a visit with Civitello's, famous for their homemade spumoni and Italian pastries. In the fall, participate in the annual Little Italy Street Fest when the neighborhood buzzes with music, games, and yummy food. Schenectady's Little Italy is a genuine slice of Italian heritage that will captivate your senses. Check the Facebook page for the date and details.

TIP

Learn more about the Italian American experience at the American Italian Heritage Museum and Cultural Center. This repository showcases photos and artifacts and serves as a gathering place for community events.

1227 Central Ave., 518-435-1979
americanitalianmuseum.org

More Perreca's
31 N Jay St., Schenectady, 518-377-9800
perrecas.com

Cornells in Little Italy
39 N Jay St., Schenectady, 518-630-5002
cornellsitalian.com

Civitello's
42 N Jay St., Schenectady, 518-381-6165
civitellos.com

facebook.com/littleitalystreetfest

Guptill's Roller-Skating Arena

MUSIC
AND ENTERTAINMENT

TIPTOE THROUGH THE TULIP FESTIVAL
IN WASHINGTON PARK

Welcome spring with the annual Tulip Festival at Washington Park, a weekend-long grand celebration of Mother's Day. Begin on Friday at the street-scrubbing ceremony on State Street, referencing the Dutch tradition of purifying streets before a great festivity. This ceremonial kickoff has marked the start of the Tulip Festival for over seven decades, inviting everyone to participate in the joyous occasion. Continue the celebrations at Washington Park, where more than 100,000 tulips bloom in stunning colors, creating a mesmerizing spectacle. The park, graced with lovely footbridges, statues, and a serene lake, comes alive with art exhibits, live performances, craft vendors, and a dedicated kids' zone. Be sure to witness the coronation of the Tulip Queen, a tradition honoring local women for their community service.

Washington Park, 518-434-4524
washingtonparkconservancy.org

TIP

Tulip gardens bloom for weeks, before and after the Tulip Festival. Follow #518TulipTracker for time and place and check the Self-Guided Tulip & Garden Driving Map for where to see the colorful displays.
albany.org/blog/post/self-guided-tulip-garden-driving-tour

MORE POPULAR FESTIVALS AROUND ALBANY

Art on Lark
artonlark.net

Old Songs Festival
festival.oldsongs.org

PearlPalooza
downtownalbany.org/pearlpalooza

Troy Pig Out
downtowntroy.org/pig-out

Troy Victorian Stroll
victorianstroll.com

CRACK THE TALE OF THE EGG
AT THE CENTER FOR THE PERFORMING ARTS

Now, imagine this: Governor Nelson Rockefeller and architect Wally Harrison, deep in discussion over breakfast, hatch a wild plan to crack the monotony of vertical towers in Albany's skyline. The blueprint? Nothing but an overturned coffee cup and a half-eaten grapefruit. Conceived as The Meeting Center, the architectural oddity came to be known as The Egg. Initially, the idea ruffled a few official feathers, but the politicians eventually caved to public sentiment. Thus, Albany became the proud owner of the world's largest "oeuf." The transformation of The Egg into theatrical spaces is quite the Albany yarn, with credit often attributed to Mayor Erastus Corning. Built during the Rockefeller era, this exceptional structure, costing a cool $90–100 million (in 1970s money), has been both the city's pride and the subject of skepticism. Even today, performers get a chuckle out of The Egg's shape, cracking jokes and even serenading it in song, as when They Might Be Giants amusingly crooned, "From the outside, I am thinking, *what were they thinking?*"

Empire State Plaza, 518-473-1061
theegg.org

TIP
Visitor parking under the Empire State Plaza is free for 90 minutes, or at a flat rate of $10 beyond that.

GROOVE TO THE RHYTHMS
OF ALIVE AT FIVE

Boogie on down to Alive at Five, a lively concert series that brings music and excitement to Downtown Albany. As the name suggests, these free outdoor performances kick off at 5 p.m. on Thursdays throughout the summer, featuring a dynamic blend of local and national artists across various genres, from rock and country to R&B and pop. Set against the beautiful Hudson Riverfront backdrop, Alive at Five isn't just about music; it's a celebration of summer. Enjoy food and beverages from local vendors, meet new people, and dance the evening away in the golden light of the setting sun. Each concert promises a memorable evening full of toe-tapping music, friendly faces, and shoreline sunset. Alive at Five is your ticket to summertime joy, laughter, and good tunes.

Jennings Landing, 1 Quay St., 518-434-2489
albanyevents.org/events/alive-at-five/

TIP
Return in September for the annual Albany Riverfront Jazz Festival, an all-day free event.
albany.org/things-to-do/events-calendar/
annual-events-and-festivals/albany-jazz-festival

RIDE THE ZIPPER
AT THE ALTAMONT FAIR

From its humble beginnings in Albany in 1819, when the first Agricultural Jubilee took place in Washington Park and the State Capitol, the fair has celebrated regional agriculture and spirit. Initially championed by the Albany Agricultural Society and featuring events like livestock displays and the occasional horse race, the fair eventually found its permanent home in Altamont. In 1893, after an ambitious public meeting the previous year, Altamont proudly hosted its first annual Albany County Fair, with harness horse racing stealing the show in front of the grandstand. Changes ensued: the grandstand became today's poultry building and the original offices made way for restrooms. As years passed and memories accumulated, thrilling attractions like the Zipper became synonymous with the fair's lively atmosphere. Today, the Altamont Fairgrounds, spanning over 138 acres, remains one of New York State's largest fair venues. Besides the carnival and the agricultural exhibits, expect to find pageants, live entertainment, the Blue Ribbon Cooking Center, and many vendors.

New York 146 and Arlington St., Guilderland, 518-861-6671
altamontfair.com

REVEL IN THE GRANDEUR
OF THE PALACE THEATRE

Experience the elegance of yesteryear and the excitement of top-tier entertainment at the Palace Theatre. An architectural marvel, this beautifully restored 1930s movie house takes you back in time with its ornate decor, grand chandeliers, and velvet curtains. But don't let the Baroque detail fool you; the Palace Theatre is a hub of modern entertainment, hosting diverse performances from rock concerts and comedy shows to classic films and ballet. With a lineup that caters to all tastes, every visit promises a unique experience. Be sure to take a moment to appreciate the intricate murals painted by Hungarian artists Andrew Karoly and Louis Szanto adorning the interior, a testament to the craftsmanship of the past. Balancing historic details with contemporary entertainment, the Palace Theatre isn't just a venue. It's an unforgettable experience that transports you to a world of glamour, culture, and artistry.

19 Clinton Ave., 518-465-3335
palacealbany.org

TIP

Check the events schedule for Albany Symphony performances at the Palace Theatre (and elsewhere around Albany, including at Proctors Theatre, EMPAC, and the Troy Savings Bank Music Hall). Under the baton of conductor David Alan Miller—a.k.a. Cowboy Dave—Albany Symphony performances range from fun family concerts to the Video Games Live event, which draws music from popular games like HALO, to a Capital Heritage series that performs works inspired by local history at the very locations that inspired them.

albanysymphony.com

HOIST A TELEPHONE POLE
AT THE CAPITAL DISTRICT
SCOTTISH GAMES

From the soul-stirring sounds of bagpipes to mighty feats of strength in traditional competitions, the Capital District Scottish Games is an entertaining ode to Scottish heritage. Don your tartans and join in the jubilation as athletes compete in the iconic caber toss, stone put, and hammer throw. But it's not just about physical prowess; the melodic harmonies of fiddles, drums, and ancient Scottish songs fill the air, evoking the spirit of the Highlands. Dance displays where performers in traditional attire leap and twirl become visual poetry. Stalls are laden with Scottish treats, while artisans showcase their Celtic crafts, tying past to present. Whether you're of Scottish descent or just admire its rich culture (or men in kilts!), these games promise a day of boisterous merriment. Dig deep into traditions that have endured and thrived, and find yourself enchanted by Scotland's legacy in America.

50 Mather Ave., Schenectady
scotgames.com

NAVIGATE THE HISTORIC HUDSON RIVER
ON DUTCH APPLE CRUISES

Step aboard Dutch Apple Cruises for an enthralling excursion along the historic Hudson River. As the river's peaceful waters ripple beneath you, this popular dayliner provides scenic vistas, engaging narration, and a warm, inviting atmosphere. Experience the enchanting beauty of the Hudson Valley's forested landscapes (incredibly gorgeous during fall foliage season), the mesmerizing city skyline, and the awe-inspiring sight of historic lighthouses. Each cruise is enriched by informative guides sharing fascinating tales and facts about the Hudson's legacy. From daytime sightseeing tours to special event party cruises, Dutch Apple offers many opportunities to soak in the stunning surroundings, from either the comfort of the enclosed climate-controlled decks or the fresh air of open upper decks. Weather permitting, the cruise season runs from April through October.

141 Broadway, 518-463-0220
dutchapplecruises.com

DO THE JITTERBUG
AT THE LINDA, WAMC'S PERFORMING ARTS STUDIO

The Linda, WAMC's Performing Arts Studio, is not just a venue; it's a platform echoing Albany's diverse voices, talents, and up-and-coming performers. Dance enthusiasts will be swayed by the infectious rhythms of the weekly swing events, providing a space to move, groove, and connect. For film lovers, their curated screenings emphasize the interplay between visuals and sound, showcasing films where music isn't just an accompaniment but an integral storyteller. If the allure of live radio captivates you, here's your chance to be part of a dynamic studio audience, experiencing firsthand the spontaneity and energy of live broadcasts. Yet, at its core, The Linda is about music. From seasoned artists who've graced numerous stages to emerging voices ready to make their mark, this is where they converge, offering a spectrum of sounds that resonate with every listener.

339 Central Ave., 518-465-5233
thelinda.org

ATTEND A PLAY
AT THE CAPITAL REPERTORY THEATRE

Capital Repertory Theatre, affectionately known as "theREP," is a 309-seat professional regional theater that serves as a centerpiece for the theatrical arts in the region. Now housed at a former Nabisco bakery after a $14 million renovation, the new digs offer an intimate and engaging environment in which to appreciate compelling performances. Capital Repertory's dedication to high-quality productions and innovative staging has become a beacon for local, national, and international talent. Notable world premieres include *Dreaming Emmett* by Toni Morrison, *Breaking Up Is Hard to Do* based on songs by Neil Sedaka, and *Grand View* by Albany-born William Kennedy. Its exceptional lineup, from classics to thought-provoking contemporary pieces, inspires dialogue, reflection, and connection.

251 N Pearl St., 518-346-6204
capitalrep.org

FUN FACT

Born in Albany in 1928, Pulitzer Prize–winning author William Kennedy set eight of his novels in Albany, including the Academy Award–nominated *Ironweed*. Capturing the city's essence through gritty realism, lyrical prose, and tales of multigenerational families, his works delve deeply into Albany's history, memory, and the unyielding spirit of its community.

WATCH A SHOW
AT THE HISTORIC COHOES MUSIC HALL

Constructed in 1874 by business tycoons, Cohoes Music Hall is a testament to a prosperous industrial past. Housing retail spaces, offices, and a 475-seat music hall, the four-story structure quickly became the heart of Cohoes's business district. Over 30 years, the music hall saw performances by legends like Buffalo Bill Cody, John Philip Sousa, and even P. T. Barnum's baby elephant, Hunky Punky. However, following financial struggles, the halls went silent in 1905 and remained so for over 60 years. The city acquired the building for a mere one dollar in 1968, sparking an ambitious restoration project that breathed new life into the dormant theater. The grand reopening in 1975—exactly a century after the original opening—brought the hall back to its glory. Today, the Cohoes Music Hall, managed by Playhouse Stage Company, is the fourth-oldest operational music hall in the US. Offering professional musical theater, the music hall continues to be a beacon of performance art and historic charm.

58 Remsen St., Cohoes, 518-434-0776
thecohoesmusichall.org

TIP

In the summer, the Playhouse Stage Company takes over at the Spanish Revival–style Lake House Amphitheater in Washington Park. For over two decades, they've been captivating audiences with a wide array of musical theater performances. With its inclusive ethos, the amphitheater offers free seating, welcoming everyone to share in these magical theater experiences.

ENJOY VINTAGE RIDES
AT HUCK FINN'S PLAYLAND

Evoke childhood memories and create new ones at Huck Finn's Playland. This sweet, toddler-friendly amusement park breathes new life into the nostalgia of the former Hoffman's Playland, a 60-year-old theme park. Relocated to the Huck Finn's Warehouse setting, the new park retains most of the rides and all the kiddie draw. Here, you can relish the timeless appeal of 18 meticulously maintained rides dating from the mid-20th century. Share a tranquil ride on the Allan Herschell merry-go-round complete with its cute chariots and carved horses arranged three abreast, reconnoiter the park from the train that circles the other rides, or ascend to new heights on the Eli Bridge Ferris wheel. Send the little ones to navigate the skies on the Red Baron planes or to drive on the "road" in teeny 4x4 trucks. Take advantage of the exhilarating spin of the classic Eli Bridge Scrambler or the Hrubetz Paratrooper. Huck Finn's Playland preserves the magic of vintage amusement for all ages.

25 Erie Blvd., 518-242-7575
facebook.com/huckfinnsplayland

TIP
Ramp up the excitement by bringing the kids to the FunPlex Fun Park. It's a popular family spot, boasting a wide variety of kid-centric activities such as mini golf, go-karts, a rock-climbing wall, batting cages, bumper boats, and even a bungee trampoline.
589 Columbia Trnpk., East Greenbush, 518-477-2651
0463126.netsolhost.com

CATCH A PERFORMANCE
AT LARK HALL

Enjoy a thrilling blend of history, music, and culture at Lark Hall. Initially built for the Masonic Daughters of the Eastern Chapter, it's a sparkling performance venue tucked inside a beautifully restored circa 1916 building. Expect an eclectic lineup of live performances, from heart-thumping rock concerts to soulful acoustic sessions. One month might include a weeklong celebration of the posthumous anniversary of Jerry Garcia's birthday, and another might be an immersive production of the rock musical *Rent*, with performers singing throughout the hall and the crowd joining in by the end. The venue's attention to acoustics and aesthetics sets it apart, with vintage tin ceilings and a balcony that overlooks the proscenium stage. Whether you're an avid music lover or just a casual visitor, the versatility and intimate charm of Lark Hall will draw you in.

351 Hudson Ave., 518-599-5804
larkhallalbany.com

Lark Street is at the center of Albany's arts and culture district. Pair a show at Lark Hall with a stop at any of the following bars:

Lark Street Tavern
453 Madison Ave., 518-650-6071
thelarkstreettavern.com

Lo-Fi Cocktail Bar & Lounge
199 Lark St., 518-621-7889
lofialbany.com

Savoy Taproom
301 Lark St., 518-599-5140
savoyonlark.com

Café Hollywood on Lark
275 Lark St., 518-472-9043
facebook.com/cafehollywoodlark

DANCE TO YOUR OWN BEAT
AT FUZE BOX

Boogie to the rhythm of the night at Fuze Box, an eclectic counterculture dance club that pulsates with high-spirited energy. With an ethos that embraces diverse music genres, it's a place where you can feel the beat from electronic dance to '80s retro and everything in between. Whether you're a dedicated clubber or a casual night owl, Fuze Box's expert DJs will have your feet moving and your heart pumping to an assortment of tunes. Its top-tier sound system and lively dance floor ensure an invigorating and unforgettable nightlife experience. The club's inclusivity welcomes all, no matter musical taste or dancing skills. After a night at Fuze Box, you'll leave with ringing ears, a joyful heart, and the electric thrum of music in your veins.

12 Central Ave.
fuzeboxalbany.com

GLIMMER WITH GIVING
AT CAPITAL HOLIDAY LIGHTS

The Capital Holiday Lights show, with its stunning array of over 125 light displays, has always been more than just a holiday tradition. This illuminating event has doubled as a holiday celebration and an annual fundraiser for the Albany Police Athletic League, Inc. (PAL). Since its twinkling inception in November 1997, Capital Lights has not only shared the magic of the season with over two million visitors but also funneled its proceeds toward the enrichment of local youth through PAL's initiatives. While the memories of its times in Washington Park still glow warmly in many hearts, 2023 brought a new chapter to this tale. The Altamont Fairgrounds now serve as the backdrop for the Capital Holiday Lights Extravaganza. With its inaugural year at the new location behind us, the revamped experience promises continuity in its mission: celebrating the season, supporting the community, and championing the future. As the lights dazzle, their shimmer echoes the legacy of giving that has always defined this event.

New York 146 and Arlington St., Guilderland, 518-435-0392
pallights.com

SPIN BACK TIME
AT GUPTILL'S ROLLER-SKATING ARENA

Swap your everyday shoes for roller skates and embrace nostalgia at Guptill's Roller-Skating Arena, proud holder of the "World's Largest Indoor Skating Rink" title since 1951. What better place to practice your twirls and show off your moonwalk glide? The arena also cradles a slice of Albany's heart, with generations of locals weaving their adolescent memories here under the spinning disco ball. Rentals are on hand, but if you want to return, consider purchasing your skates at the fully stocked shop. Whether you're a pro or a beginner, you have a spot on the glossy wooden floor. And remember to grab a snack at the vintage concession stand, where the hot dogs rival the roller skates for the title of "most-loved item."

1085 Loudon Rd., Cohoes, 518-785-0660
guptillsarena.com

TIP
After working up an appetite, saunter next door to Guptill's Ice Cream stand. With a cornucopia of pleasing flavors and a ridiculously long list of sundae toppings, this is a local favorite.

CLAIM
THE SHOTGUN SEAT
AT THE JERICHO DRIVE-IN

In 1957, the Jericho Drive-In theater opened with Rock Hudson's *Battle Hymn* on Flag Day. Nearly 70 years later, the beloved theater retains the spirit of yesteryear, albeit with technological upgrades. The auditory experience is relatively modern, thanks to FM radio sound and an AM channel for vintage vehicles, ensuring crystal-clear dialogue and music. As one of the few remaining drive-ins in America, its double features are a bargain, combining classic films with today's top box office hits. But the experience isn't just about films; there are also decadent treats. The Twist Ice Cream Shoppe elevates the usual film fare, adding frozen lemonade, cake pops, and ice cream pies to the candy and popcorn lineup. They keep the menu interesting with rotating sundae specials such as the Maple Bacon Bomb or Everything Apple with pie at its base. It's not just a movie venue; it's a trip into deliciously nostalgic Americana.

21 Jericho Rd., Glenmont, 518-767-3398
jerichodrive-in.com

MARVEL AT THE WATER SKI SHOW
AT JUMPIN' JACK'S DRIVE-IN

Experience the magic of an extraordinary water show at a classic American drive-in burger joint, Jumpin' Jack's Drive-In. As the sun dips below the horizon on a summer Tuesday night, tuck into your favorite comfort foods—juicy Jack Burgers topped with coleslaw, crispy fries, or velvety soft-serve ice cream— while the adjacent Mohawk River becomes the stage for the spectacular US Water Ski Show Team. Guided by an engaging MC, the water ski club's talented athletes command the river surface with daring stunts and precision maneuvers. This is the same team that counts as part of its legacy a 1986 *Guinness Book of World Records* feat that sent nine men over a small ski jump and, in 1994, a "monster pyramid" comprising a four-tier pyramid flanked by two three-tier pyramids performed live on TV. Watch, enthralled, as they carve intricate paths, execute flawless formations, and build astonishing human pyramids, all at breathtaking speeds.

5 Schonowee Ave., Scotia, 518-393-6101
jumpinjacksdriveininc.com

TUNE IN TO
GILDED AGE GOLD
AT THE TROY SAVINGS BANK

Picture yourself in a concert hall where legends like Dizzy Gillespie, Yo-Yo Ma, and even Mark Twain once held sway, a space so acoustically perfect that a hushed whisper can touch every ear. That's the Troy Savings Bank Music Hall. The room is an architectural marvel—with a sloped stage, original seating, box seats, and an impressive chandelier—all contributing to the perfection of musical performances. But the building's history is as illustrious as its design. The Troy Chromatics, once the Chromatics Club, held their inaugural concert here in 1902 with Metropolitan Opera soprano Lillian Nordica, and the most recent iteration of the Chromatics group continues to play the venue to this day. This harmonious relationship led the way for various luminaries to grace the stage—pianist Vladimir Horowitz, contralto Marian Anderson, and pianist Arthur Rubinstein, among others. In Troy Music Hall, every corner is steeped in history and every note is swathed in superb acoustics, offering a concert and a symphony where the past and present engage in a timeless duet.

30 2nd St., Troy, 518-273-0038
troymusichall.org

TIP

Look for the Troy Savings Bank Music Hall in Season One of the HBO series *Gilded Age* where it is used to portray the Academy of Music.

HEDGE YOUR BETS
AT THE SARATOGA RACE COURSE

Gather your friends, don your best hat, and enter the heart-pounding world of thoroughbred racing at the Saratoga Race Course. Revered as one of the oldest sporting venues in the US, it's where equine athleticism meets adrenaline-fueled excitement. This grande dame of American horse racing springs to life each summer, hosting six weeks of top-tier contests that draw international attention. Feel your heart race in sync with the thunderous gallop of hooves as you witness horses and jockeys vying for glory in iconic races like the Travers Stakes. Beyond the racing, indulge in the timeless tradition of a picnic in the backyard, or explore the National Museum of Racing and Hall of Fame nearby. The Saratoga Race Course is a rite of summer that's steeped in tradition and an exhilarating spectacle that never fails to thrill.

267 Union Ave., Saratoga Springs, 518-584-6200
nyra.com/saratoga

TIP

Arrive early, between 7–9:30 a.m., for Breakfast at the Track on the Porch of the Clubhouse and if you want to take advantage of the free Backstretch tour, opt for the first tram of the day as they are usually less crowded. There's also a fascinating Breeding Farm Tour, but those tend to book up as soon as reservations become available in the spring.

RACE THE FAST AND FURIOUS
AT LEBANON VALLEY SPEEDWAY

Fuel your adrenaline rush at Lebanon Valley Speedway, where thunderous engines and smoking tires create an unforgettable spectacle on the half-mile, high-banked, clay oval. Home to high-octane dirt track racing, this famous speedway serves up thrilling races and daring passes that leave spectators on the edges of their seats. From April to October, the dust clouds and the roaring of engines become the speedway's heartbeat as various classes, including Modifieds, Pro Stocks, and Street Stocks, go wheel-to-wheel in pursuit of victory. The speedway also features a quarter-mile dragway, where drivers can test their street vehicles on Wednesday nights. Whether you're a motorsport fan or seeking a new adventure, Lebanon Valley Speedway provides a unique blend of entertainment and excitement. Speed is the language in this arena, and exhilaration is the norm.

1746 US-20, West Lebanon, 518-794-9606
lebanonvalley.com
dragway.com

Empire State Plaza Ice Rink

SPORTS
AND RECREATION

GLIDE ACROSS
THE EMPIRE STATE PLAZA ICE RINK

Slip on your skates and glide through winter at the Empire State Plaza Ice Rink. This outdoor rink, framed by towering buildings and sparkling lights, makes for a picturesque and exhilarating experience. At 123 feet by 112 feet, the rink offers plenty of room for spins, turns, and leisurely coasting, no matter your skill level. Whether you're a seasoned pro or strapping on skates for the first time, the ice rink promises laughter and memorable moments. Warm up with a cup of hot cocoa from the snack bar or capture the perfect winter selfie with the iconic Egg performing arts center as your backdrop. Rentals are available on-site, so you only need a sense of adventure. Open from December to March, it's an enchanting way to savor the winter season.

Empire State Plaza, 518-473-6299
empirestateplaza.ny.gov

TIP

Skating at night or on weekends? Find plenty of free street parking on State Street next to the Empire State Plaza.

MORE GREAT ICE-SKATING RINKS

ICE SKATING OUTDOORS

Buckingham Pond
Berkshire Blvd.
buckinghampondconservancy.org

Washington Park Lake
613 Madison Ave., 518-434-4524
washingtonparkconservancy.org

Swinburne Park
810 Clinton Ave., 518-434-5699
albanyny.gov/879/rec-centers

INDOOR ICE-SKATING RINKS

Albany County Hockey Facility
830 Albany Shaker Rd., 518-452-7396
albanycounty.com/departments/recreation/hockey-facility

Bethlehem Ice Rink
900 Delaware Ave., Delmar, 518-439-4394
cdymca.org/locations/bethlehem-ymca/bethlehem-ice-rink

SPOT AN ENDANGERED BUTTERFLY
AT THE PINE BUSH PRESERVE

Shift from the bustling urban sprawl of Albany to the serene, sandy trails of Pine Bush Preserve. Covering a sprawling 3,300 acres, this ecological gem is a guardian of the rare inland pine barrens ecosystem. As you traverse its undulating dunes, notice the whispering pitch pines and scrub oaks that shelter countless species, including the elusive endangered Karner blue butterfly. With 20 miles of trails at your disposal, you'll meander through habitats dotted with blue lupines, shrubs, and tufts of grasses, each corner teeming with its little universe of flora and fauna. Swing by the visitor center, where hands-on exhibits weave tales of the preserve's rich history and intricate biology. The Pine Bush beckons year-round, whether you're lacing up hiking boots or strapping on snowshoes—experience nature's rhythms in Albany's backyard.

195 New Karner Rd., 518-456-0655
albanypinebush.org

ROOT
FOR THE ALBANY FIREWOLVES LACROSSE TEAM

Rally behind the Albany FireWolves, a team deeply embedded in the historical legacy of lacrosse. A relative newcomer to Albany—2023 was just the team's second season as the Albany FireWolves and its seventh season in the National Lacrosse League—the team was off to a rocky start at the MVP Arena, ending the season in second-to-last position. Still, there's much to admire in the team's proud acknowledgment of the sport's Native American origins, which traces back to the Six Nations of the Haudenosaunee Confederacy. Recognized as The Medicine Game, integral to Northeastern Native American communities, the wolf embodies fundamental values of courage, strength, loyalty, and leadership. Meanwhile, "fire" pays homage to the Mohican tribes' word for the region, Pempotowwuthut-Muhhcanneuw, which means "the fireplace of the Mohican nation." Cheer on the FireWolves as they unite the community in spirited competition, celebrating lacrosse's rich heritage while positively impacting the Capital Region.

albanyfirewolves.com

JOIN THE ALBANY ROWING CENTER
AND CREW THE HUDSON

Discover the exhilarating world of rowing at the Albany Rowing Center. Here, the rhythmic pulse of oars slicing through the Hudson River's tranquil waters is a workout and a transformative experience combining fitness, nature, and camaraderie. With programs suitable for all age groups, you'll quickly grasp the fundamentals of rowing—mastering stroke techniques, handling boats with confidence, and understanding water safety—under the guidance of expert coaches. Engage your muscles and feel the shell glide smoothly over the water, turning effort into momentum. Embrace the spirit of teamwork as you coordinate strokes with fellow rowers, experiencing the thrill of moving in unison. Taste the rush of competition by participating in regattas and feel the satisfaction of pushing your physical limits. Beyond the physical engagement, the center introduces you to a community of enthusiasts, fostering friendships forged in the shared love of this timeless sport.

Albany Rowing Center Boathouse at the Hudson River Corning Preserve
albanyrowingcenter.org

TIP
Upstate Kayak Rentals provides a self-serve kayak rental here and at 12 more locations around the region, in addition to two staffed locations.
upstatekayakrentals.com/index.html

CHEER FOR
THE ALBANY ALL STARS ROLLER DERBY

Get to know the high-energy sport of roller derby with the Albany All Stars, Albany's first women's flat-track roller derby league. Founded in 2006, this grassroots organization combines athleticism, strategy, and a dash of drama for a thrilling spectator experience. The team prides itself on inclusivity, welcoming skaters of all shapes, sizes, and skill levels to join the action or cheer from the sidelines. Watch as skaters gracefully glide, strategically block, and deftly dodge their way around the track, demonstrating strength, agility, and teamwork. Get lost in the whirlwind of fast-paced bouts, pumping music, and the electric atmosphere created by a crowd of passionate fans. The Albany All Stars deliver an exciting roller derby game and actively contribute to their community through volunteering and local partnerships.

Washington Avenue Armory, 195 Washington Ave.
albanyallstars.com

TIP
Albany All Stars Roller Derby events take place at the historic Washington Avenue Armory Sports and Convention Arena where you can also attend Albany Patroons basketball games.
albanypatroonsbasketball.com

CRUISE THE GATEWAY
TO THE ERIE CANAL

Travel back to the roots of American innovation with a visit to the starting point of the legendary Erie Canal in Albany. This engineering marvel, stretching 363 miles to Buffalo, was constructed between 1817 and 1825 under the direction of New York Governor DeWitt Clinton. Walk along the canal's paths where mules once hauled barges, visit locks crafted by yesteryear's artisans, and absorb the canal's history from informative exhibits. Today, the Erie Canal combines a rich history with leisurely recreation. You can walk or bike along the canal paths, enjoy a boat ride on the water, or revel in the picturesque scenery. A day spent exploring the Erie Canal's birthplace is a look into a crucial chapter of American history. Challenge yourself to paddle the Waterford Flight of Locks. Bypassing Cohoes Falls, this flight achieves the highest elevation (169 feet) in the shortest distance (1.5 miles) in canal locks. Kayak rental and shuttle service are available from Upstate Kayak Rentals.

Harbor Visitor Center, 1 Tugboat Alley, Waterford, 518-233-9123
town.waterford.ny.us/harbor-visitors-center.html
upstatekayakrentals.com/traveling-adventures.html

LEAF PEEP UNDER A WATERFALL
AT THACHER PARK

Gorgeous anytime, the falls present a flamboyant spectacle at John Boyd Thacher State Park. Begin your exploration at the visitor center where interactive displays explain the park's rich history and geology. Then, venture onto the famed Indian Ladder Trail. Here, you can hike under a waterfall and feel the thrilling chill of the mist against your face. The park's soaring cliffs provide a majestic frame for the riotous hues of fall, with views that stretch over vast fields and dense forests. Patrons can find easy access to the stunning view from the park's short-term parking lot, but for the best vantage point, hike the Hang Glider's Cliff trail to High Point. Thacher Park in autumn is a brilliant tapestry of nature's most stunning artistry.

830 Thacher Park Rd., Voorheesville, 518-872-1237
parks.ny.gov/parks/thacher

TIP
Save on admission fees at this, and 250 more, New York State parks. Purchase the wallet-sized Empire Pass card online, good for one to five seasons, or even for a lifetime.
ny.gov/services/get-empire-pass

CONQUER WINTER
AT MAPLE SKI RIDGE

Just a snowball's throw from Downtown Albany, the beginner-friendly Maple Ski Ridge offers the perfect introduction to skiing for young adventurers and families. Avoid the rush at larger ski resorts and enjoy this intimate mountain setting, ideal for novices seeking to master the art of the descent. Maple Ridge facilitates skill-building with their six-week lessons and winter vacation programs, and they even offer summer camps in the offseason. Their flexible ski rentals, available by day or season, make your snowy escapade easy and affordable. Add an enchanting twist to your winter evenings with their night skiing option. And if you prefer the tranquility of the trails over the rush of the slopes, join in Nordic Nights every Monday for an invigorating round of snowshoeing, cross-country skiing, or skinning. Maple Ski Ridge is both accessible and convenient for skiers of all skill levels.

2725 Mariaville Rd., Schenectady, 518-381-4700
mapleskiridge.com

SLIDE INTO ACTION
AT THE ALBANY CURLING CLUB

Feel the excitement of the ancient winter sport of curling, beautifully preserved and brought to life at the Albany Curling Club. This institution has served as a hub for the sport since 1955, offering a gripping experience that melds strategy, skill, and teamwork. Step onto the ice and feel the thrill of launching the curling stone toward the target, using finesse and precision. Feel the adrenaline rush as you work with your team, sweeping the ice with purpose and intent to influence the stone's path. Take the opportunity to attend Open House events where you can observe games, learn about the sport's intriguing rules and strategies, and understand why it has fascinated people for centuries. Curling at the Albany Curling Club isn't just about the sport itself but also encompasses the pleasure of shared experiences. After a game, socialize off the ice, exchanging stories and strategies.

117 W McKown Rd., 518-456-6272
albanycurlingclub.org

ROAM
THE INSPIRING HUDSON RIVER ART TRAIL

Experience a trek through beauty, history, and culture along the Hudson River Art Trail. From the riverside vistas that inspired a school of painters to the stunning landscapes that continue to enchant artists today, the trail winds through a breathtaking panorama of natural beauty. Stroll the same grounds that Hudson River School artists Thomas Cole and Frederic Church once roamed, sketching and painting iconic scenes that still captivate us today. Travel to Catskill, where Thomas Cole, the founder of the Hudson River School, lived and painted. Stand in the same spots where these artists once stood, watching the interplay of light and shadow and feeling the same inspiration that led to their masterpieces. A must-see highlight is the majestic Kaaterskill Falls. Once a popular subject for the school's painters, the falls tumble in two tiers over a dramatic cliff, providing an awe-inspiring sight. Walking the Hudson River Art Trail offers a unique blend of art, nature, and history that promises a memorable journey.

Hudson River School Art Trail
hudsonriverschool.org/hudsonriverschoolarttrail

Kaaterskill Falls
103 Laurel House Rd., Haines Falls, 518-357-2161

Thomas Cole National Historic Site
218 Spring St., Catskill, 518-943-7465
thomascole.org

Olana State Historic Site
5720 NY-9G, Hudson, 518-828-1872
olana.org

MORE BEAUTIFUL WATERFALLS NEAR ALBANY

Cohoes Falls
Falls View Park, 231–341 N Mohawk St., Cohoes, 518-233-2119

Minelot Falls
Thacher State Park
830 Thacher Park Rd., Voorheesville, 518-872-1237
parks.ny.gov/parks/thacher

Barberville Falls
23 Blue Factory Rd., Poestenkill, 518-712-9211
rensselaerplateau.org/barbervillefalls

Rensselaerville Falls
Huyck Preserve and Biological Research Station
5052 Delaware Trnpk., Rensselaerville, 518-797-3440
huyckpreserve.org

HIKE INTO HISTORY
AT PEEBLES ISLAND STATE PARK

Uncover the raw remnants of the American Revolution at Peebles Island State Park, where earthworks suggest tales of a tumultuous past. Indeed, these mounds, or breastworks, are tangible evidence of an era when they served as a critical line of defense. This park, situated on one of several islets formed by the Mohawk River's four "spruyts" as it blends into the Hudson, is far more than an outdoor museum. Its tranquility is as remarkable as its history, with winding trails that traverse diverse landscapes, from river shorelines to lush woods, providing ample opportunities to spot local wildlife. Peebles Island State Park provides a confluence of history—a reminder of our nation's origin—with the unspoiled beauty of nature. This destination offers visitors a step back in time and a stroll through serene surroundings.

1 Delaware Ave. N, Cohoes, 518-268-2188
parks.ny.gov/parks/peeblesisland

STAY FOR THE FIREWORKS
AT A TRI-CITY VALLEYCATS GAME

Get ready for peanuts, Cracker Jacks, and home runs as you join the fan club for the Tri-City ValleyCats! These guys joined the independent Frontier League in 1921, and they know how to put on an exciting game day. The action isn't just on the field, though. Look out for SouthPaw, the team's fun-loving mascot, who is always up to some antics to keep the crowd hyped. And let's not forget about those classic fan games between the innings. Afterward, stay for the fireworks, usually staged once a week on weekends. Whether they're knocking it out of the park or making a slick double play, watching the ValleyCats is as all-American as apple pie. So, grab your ball cap and mitt because you never know when a fly ball will come your way. After one night at the "Joe" (Joseph L. Bruno Stadium), you'll see why ValleyCats games are a local favorite.

Joseph L. Bruno Stadium, Hudson Valley Community College
80 Vandenburgh Ave., Troy, 518-629-2287
tcvalleycats.com

PEDAL THROUGH NEW YORK'S HERITAGE
ON THE EMPIRE STATE TRAIL

Stretching over 750 miles, the Empire State Trail is a cyclist's dream. As you traverse this paved pathway, you'll encounter a beautiful mix of New York scenery: riverbanks, historic canal trails, lush farmlands, and small-town charm. You'll witness history firsthand as the trail takes you past grand architectural structures, industrial relics, and natural wonders. Dotted with rest stops, food stations, and interpretive signage, the well-marked trail ensures you can ride as far as you wish without worry. Whether you're a casual rider or a seasoned cyclist, the Empire State Trail offers an unparalleled opportunity to engage with New York's rich heritage while indulging in the simple pleasure of a bike ride. An 11-mile section from Albany to Cohoes starts at the Corning Preserve or you can opt for the seven-mile Mohawk-Hudson Bike-Hike Trail (MHBHT) which is ideal for families and leisurely rides.

empiretrail.ny.gov

TIP

Convenient parking is available at the Corning Preserve, the Hudson-Mohawk Bike-Hike Trail (MHBHT) lot in Watervliet, Cannon Street in Green Island, or Peebles Island State Park, with visitor services accessible just off the trail, enhancing this urban-meets-natural cycling experience.

FLOAT DOWN THE BATTENKILL
ON A TUBING ADVENTURE

Lean back, relax, and let the gentle currents of the Battenkill take you on a tubing journey like no other. Known for its clear water and lush scenery, this tranquil river offers the perfect setting for a leisurely afternoon. The historic Battenkill, a 59.4-mile-long river that gracefully winds from Vermont into New York, is the longest eastern tributary of the Hudson River. "Kill" is the Dutch word for "creek," a fitting name for this serene waterway. As you float downstream, you'll encounter light rapids that add a hint of excitement without overwhelming the tranquil ambiance. Wildlife sightings from playful otters to soaring bald eagles provide an incredible spectacle and connect you with the natural environment. The cool water around you maintains the perfect temperature balance for comfort as the sun warms your skin. So, grab a tube, kick back, and let the river guide your way to relaxation.

Battenkill Valley Outdoors
1414 State Rte. 313, Cambridge, 518-677-3311
battenkillvalleyoutdoors.com

EXTRACT SWEET CHEMISTRY
AT THE SUGAR SHACKS

Learn about New York's rich maple syrup heritage with a visit to one of the region's sugar shacks. Tucked among the US's largest concentration of tappable maple trees, these humble cabins encapsulate the timeless art of syrup making. Here, you'll witness the transformation of sap to syrup—an additive-free sweetener produced in New York. Second only to Vermont, the state's distinct climate and robust forestry set the stage for this delicious confection. The resulting gourmet syrup and granulated sugar are symbols of tradition and pride, delicious necessities in any discerning kitchen. A visit to a sugar shack, such as the one at Mountain Winds Farm, is an immersion in local heritage, where the community's warmth matches the syrup's sweetness.

New York Pure Maple
Find a map of sugar shacks, recipes, and more on the NYS Maple Producers Association website.
nysmaple.com

Mountain Winds Farm
12 Williamson Rd., Berne
518-872-0513

TIP
Looking to buy high-quality maple syrup? Consider the grade. Maple syrup grades range from Golden (with a delicate taste, typically produced earlier in the sugaring season) to Dark (with a robust flavor, made later in the season).

SUNBATHE ON THE BEACH
AT GRAFTON LAKES STATE PARK

In the summer, soak in the sun at Grafton Lakes State Park. Boasting six pristine lakes spread out over 2,500 acres, including one lake with a beautiful sandy beach, Grafton offers many quiet corners. This New York state park is perfect for those seeking respite from city life and an opportunity to reconnect with nature. Unwind on the inviting shores of the public beach, where grains of sand weave a warm blanket beneath your toes and the gentle lap of waves becomes your tranquil soundtrack. Take out a kayak or stand-up paddleboard to explore the lakes' secluded nooks, or simply enjoy a rejuvenating dip in the clean, cool waters. As the sun sets, let the enchanting hues reflected in the waters keep you captivated. Return in winter for outstanding ice fishing and snowshoeing around the lakes.

254 Grafton Lakes State Park Way, Grafton, 518-279-1155
parks.ny.gov/parks/graftonlakes

TIP

The L.L. Bean Outdoor Discovery Programs runs several courses at Grafton Lakes including archery, fly fishing, kayaking, skishoeing, snowshoeing, standup paddleboarding, as well as orienteering and first-aid classes.

llbeanoutdoors.com/grafton-lakes-new-york

MORE LAKES AROUND ALBANY

Rensselaer Lake
Six Mile Waterworks Park
135 Fuller Rd., 518-434-5300
dec.ny.gov/outdoor/65369.html

Cherry Plain State Park
10 State Park Rd., Petersburgh, 518-733-5400
parks.ny.gov/parks/cherryplain/maps.aspx

Brown's Beach on Saratoga Lake
511 NY-9P, Saratoga Springs, 518-664-6148
stillwaterny.org/departments/parks-recreational/browns-beach-2

Thompson's Lake—Thacher State Park
68 Thompsons Lake Rd., East Berne, 518-872-1674
parks.ny.gov/parks/99/details.aspx

Moreau Lake State Park Beach
605 Old Saratoga Rd., Gansevoort, 518-793-0511
parks.ny.gov/parks/moreaulake/details.aspx

Million Dollar Beach on Lake George
139 Beach Rd., Lake George, 518-668-3352
dec.ny.gov/outdoor/113215.html

STRIDE THROUGH SNOWY TRAILS
AT FIVE RIVERS

Winter at Five Rivers Environmental Education Center transforms the landscape into a serene snow-blanketed wonderland, making it a top destination for snowshoeing enthusiasts. Across its expansive 450 acres, the gentle crunch of snowshoes punctuates the hush, guiding adventurers from frosty wetlands to silent, snow-draped forests. For newcomers, the well-marked trails offer an introduction to this stimulating winter activity, while experienced trekkers can deepen their connection with nature amid the center's tranquil settings. Should you need a break, the interpretive center becomes a warm haven, providing educational insights into the park's ecosystems. While snowshoeing, watch for animal tracks or the occasional winter bird, offering hints of the lively world beneath the snow. Whether seeking a workout, solace in nature, or a frosty adventure, snowshoeing at Five Rivers promises a magical winter experience. Access is free, but there is a small fee for snowshoe rentals (available when there are more than six inches of snow on the ground).

56 Game Farm Rd., Delmar, 518-475-0291
dec.ny.gov/education/1835.html

TIP

Snowshoe or cross-country ski in the foothills of the Taconic Mountains on Pineridge Cross-Country Ski Area trails. Rentals and lessons available for both, day pass fee required.

1463 Plank Rd., Petersburgh, 518-283-3652
pineridgexc.com

RUN THE HAIRY GORILLA HALF MARATHON
OR SQUIRRELLY SIX MILE

Join the hilariously wild and exhilarating Hairy Gorilla Half Marathon, where it's as much about having fun as it is about the run. Each October, the event occurs on a gnarly trail at Thacher State Park, blending Halloween spirit with intense trail running. The race organizers have a wacky sense of humor, so be prepared for a race like no other. Not up for a half-marathon? No problem. The Squirrelly Six Mile race offers a shorter but equally entertaining option. In both events, runners are encouraged to wear outrageous costumes. You might see witches, zombies, and, yes, even hairy gorillas dashing through the woods. The course can be as tricky as a werewolf navigating a silverware drawer, with a mix of steep hills and winding trails. But hey, who says you can't have a few laughs while pushing your endurance limits? The Hairy Gorilla Half Marathon and Squirrelly Six Mile are more than just races; they're a wild romp through the woods you won't forget!

hairygorillahalf.com

TIP
Find more races and social runs on the Albany Running Exchange.
albanyrunningexchange.org

STEP UP TO BAT
AT THE BASEBALL HALL OF FAME

America's beloved sport is enshrined in the Baseball Hall of Fame. This is more than a museum; it's a narrative unfolding, encapsulating the game's joys, heartaches, victories, and evolution. With every turn, find an epic tale of athletic prowess and tenacity. Explore the *Sacred Ground* exhibit showcasing the history and unique architecture of some of the more illustrious stadiums. Wander through *The Souls of the Game: Voices of Black Baseball* to understand the critical role of African American players in shaping the game. See the *Autumn Glory* section, commemorating all the World Series champions and their roads to triumph. Learn about the courageous women who broke barriers in this male-dominated sport in *Diamond Dreams*. Capture a piece of the action in the interactive *Whole New Ballgame* exhibit, which tells the story of the last five decades in baseball. The Baseball Hall of Fame, rich with artifacts, stories, and heritage, is a testament to the unifying spirit of the game—an essential visit for any sports enthusiast.

25 Main St., Cooperstown, 888-425-5633
baseballhall.org

JOURNEY TO THE CENTER OF THE EARTH
AT HOWE CAVERNS

Dare to go into the subterranean depths of Howe Caverns, a six-million-year-old, prehistoric underground labyrinth. Stretching over 150 feet below the earth's surface, this network of limestone corridors, immense boulders, and shimmering mineral-laden walls offers an experience like no other. Discover the stalactites and stalagmites, with names like the Giant Formation and the Pipe Organ, and learn the stories behind their centuries-long formation. The temperature remains at 52 degrees Fahrenheit, making it a year-round adventure. Tread undulating pathways to Titan's Temple, the largest room, and float aboard a boat on the tranquil underground lake that is part of the meandering cavern stream known as the River Styx, so clear it mirrors the ceiling above. Adding to the thrill is the walk through the Winding Way, a serpentine passage through narrow gaps that adds an element of suspense. Howe Caverns is a journey of geological beauty, a historical spectacle that combines adventure with a touch of science, perfect for thrill seekers and geology buffs alike.

255 Discovery Dr., Howes Cave, 518-296-8900
howecaverns.com

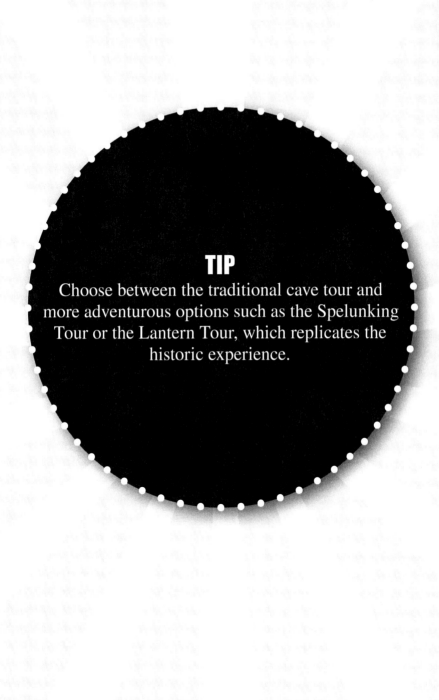

TIP
Choose between the traditional cave tour and more adventurous options such as the Spelunking Tour or the Lantern Tour, which replicates the historic experience.

Nipper

CULTURE
AND HISTORY

CHASE A LOVE STORY
AT THE SCHUYLER MANSION

Study a timeless romance at the Schuyler Mansion, the grand home of General Philip Schuyler, and more significantly, the backdrop of Alexander Hamilton's courtship of a Van Rensselaer heiress. Embrace your inner *Hamilton* fan and follow the trail of their engagement throughout the 18th-century Georgian mansion. Be awed by the carefully restored interiors of the home where they were wed, check out the desk where the Founding Father penned some of the *Federalist Papers*, stroll the gardens where whispered promises might have been exchanged, or join a guided tour for a deeper insight. Time your outing for the spring, and you could attend the annual Pinkster Festival. Once a Dutch observation of Pentecost, this event morphed into a celebration by enslaved and free Africans, enabling them to maintain cultural traditions. Visiting Schuyler Mansion is an embrace of both poignant love and layered history.

32 Catherine St., 518-434-0834
parks.ny.gov/historic-sites/schuylermansion/details.aspx

HAMILTON WALKING TOUR

Add the **Schuyler Mansion** to a self-guided walking tour
in Alexander Hamilton's footsteps:

Start at the **Albany Visitors Center** in Quackenbush Square
for a history lesson.
25 Quackenbush Sq., 518-434-1217
albany.org/about/visitors-center

Toss back a pint at **The Olde English Pub** where
Colonel Quackenbush stopped for refreshments when escorting
a British prisoner to Schuyler Mansion in 1777.
683 Broadway, 518-434-6533
theoldeenglish.com

Visit the **First Church** where a eulogy upon Hamilton's death
spurred the outlawing of duels.
110 N Pearl St., 518-463-4449
firstchurchinalbany.org

After the duel, Aaron Burr is said to have stayed at the
Fort Orange Club when it was still a boarding house.
Nowadays, you'll need a member's invitation or reciprocal
club membership to visit.
110 Washington Ave., 518-434-2101
fortorangeclub.com

GAZE AT PRISTINE WILDERNESS
IN THE ALBANY INSTITUTE OF HISTORY & ART

Witness the Hudson Valley's once-untouched wilderness through the eyes of early conservationist and artist Thomas Cole and artists from the renowned Hudson River School art movement. Every piece tells a story of nature's grandeur and man's relation to it; find the most extensive collection of these landscapes at the Albany Institute of History & Art. Founded in 1791, it's one of America's oldest museums. The museum's architecture is a journey, with sections like the opulent Beaux-Arts mansion coexisting harmoniously alongside a sleek contemporary wing, effortlessly bridging the past and present. Discover artifacts from Ancient Egypt, remnants of early Dutch settlers, and thematic rotating exhibits as you meander through its halls. Whether it's toys, intricate shoes, or the latest outerwear collection, each show illustrates the historical fabric of Albany and the Upper Hudson Valley.

125 Washington Ave., 518-463-4478
albanyinstitute.org

BEHOLD THE GIANT DOG
IN THE SKY

A 28-foot, four-ton terrier towering over the landscape is an arresting sight. This isn't just any dog—it's *Nipper*, the faithful RCA mascot, who has watched over Albany's skyline from the top of the historic American Meter Company building since 1958. A testament to past industry, *Nipper* is now a beacon, visible from five miles away, amid the vibrant warehouse district's revitalization. Remember, you don't need a ticket or a tour—lift your eyes to the sky, and there he is, waiting for your wave. Extend your *Nipper* tour by seeking out his mini replicas, remnants of the "Downtown Is Pawsome" public art installation. From *Capital Canines* at The Olde English Pub to *Bloomie* by the Hudson River Way Pedestrian Bridge, these colorful statues pay homage to Albany's colossal canine and infuse an extra dash of charm to the city's landscape.

Nipper statue
991 Broadway

"DOWNTOWN IS PAWSOME" ART INSTALLATION
Capital Canines, 683 Broadway
Cleeo of Clee Park, 110 N Pearl St.
Happy Puppy, N Pearl Street and Clinton Ave.
Industrial Anthropology, 25 Orange St. (north side of building)
Awaken, 25 Orange St.
Up Above!, 144 State St.
Bloomie at Hudson River Way Pedestrian Bridge

SHINE A LIGHT ON HISTORY
AT THE UNDERGROUND RAILROAD EDUCATION CENTER

Revisit an era of clandestine courage at the Underground Railroad Education Center. This remarkable institution resides in the Stephen and Harriet Myers Residence, a beacon of bravery during tumult and trepidation. From the 1825 completion of the Erie Canal, Albany blossomed as a hub for riverboat shipping, creating a bustling backdrop for Underground Railroad operations. Here, the era's emerging transportation systems and social movements provided fertile ground for networking, which was crucial in assisting freedom seekers on their path to liberty. Learn about the unsung heroes who dared to defy federal statutes for the cause of freedom. Stand in awe of figures like Stephen Myers, a journalist who helped many escape slavery; William Henry Johnson, an unyielding abolitionist; and the courageous Mott sisters, Abigail and Lydia, pillars of the local Quaker community. Visiting the Underground Railroad Education Center is an opportunity to learn how the quest for freedom shaped Albany's history.

194 Livingston Ave., 518-621-7793
undergroundrailroadhistory.org

FIND FAMOUS AMERICANS
AT THE ALBANY RURAL CEMETERY

For a peaceful promenade steeped in history, look no further than Albany Rural Cemetery. This tranquil oasis serves as a memorial park, arboretum, and open-air museum, where the whispers of times past echo through this sacred burial ground. Spanning over 400 acres, this historic cemetery nestles in a rolling landscape adorned with centuries-old trees and intricate 19th-century funerary art. Thousands of gravestones, monuments, and mausoleums line the picturesque trails, each telling a unique story of Albany's past residents. Prominent figures reside here for eternity, including one president and several senators, congressmen, governors, soldiers, inventors, and artists. Among these is the 21st US president, Chester A. Arthur, whose angel-guarded grave offers a contemplative spot for history buffs. Whether exploring the verdant grounds or tracing Albany's rich historical legacy, Albany Rural Cemetery provides a serene retreat from the rush of modern life.

3 Cemetery Ave., 518-463-7017
albanyruralcemetery.org

TIP

Equally tranquil is the Oakwood Cemetery. Spanning 282 acres, its hillsides are dotted with winding roads, elaborate mausoleums, and stunning views of the Hudson Valley. Check the website for a wide variety of events, from live concerts to Full Moon Twilight Tours.

50 101st St., Troy, 518-272-7520
oakwoodcemetery.org

EXPLORE EPOCHS
AT THE NEW YORK STATE MUSEUM

Travel through time at the New York State Museum, an immense treasure trove showcasing art, history, and natural wonders. Holding a colossal collection of over 16 million artifacts, each corner of the museum unfurls a new lesson. Stand in awe of the Cohoes Mastodon, a majestic reminder of the Ice Age. Dig deeper into Earth's past with exhibits such as *Beneath the City*, which uncovers the ancient, fossilized creatures found during the New York City subway construction. Uncover the state's geological past in *A Small Window into the Earth's History*, which highlights unique rock formations and mineral deposits. Wander through the life-size Iroquois longhouse, a recreation of the traditional dwellings that once dotted New York State, offering a glimpse into the rich culture of the Iroquois Confederacy. Discovery Place is a special place for children, where hands-on experiences with science and nature inspire young minds. The New York State Museum is a haven for history buffs and aspiring naturalists.

222 Madison Ave., 518-474-5877
nysm.nysed.gov

TIP

Be sure to make your way to the fourth floor, where a beautifully restored Herschell-Spillman carousel awaits riders every hour on the hour between 11 a.m and 4 p.m. Interestingly, although the carousel was built in 1914, its animals are even older. Hand-carved in Brooklyn in 1895 by an immigrant German toymaker, they're among the oldest carousel animals in the country.

ADMIRE
STYLE SIMPLICITY
AT THE SHAKER HERITAGE SOCIETY

Transport yourself into a world of peace, simplicity, and innovative design at the Shaker Heritage Society. Founded in 1776 as America's first Shaker settlement, this National Historic District beautifully embodies the Shakers' vision of a heavenly society on earth, marked by equality, pacifism, and communal living. Visit the sacred halls of the meticulously preserved 1848 Meeting House, where the Shakers held their spiritual dances, the spectacle that earned them their name. The Shakers' innovative spirit continues to shine in structures like the Brethren's Workshop, a testament to its skilled craftsmanship and innovative designs. See the heritage herb garden, a nod to the Shakers' trailblazing work in herbal remedies and seed saving. Inside the repurposed 1915 Barn, you'll find a museum filled with exhibits showcasing the Shakers' innovative agricultural tools, elegantly simple furniture, and handmade crafts. Finally, attend one of their seasonal craft fairs or history-themed events. With every visit, you'll leave the Shaker Heritage Society with a deeper appreciation for this unique slice of American history and culture.

25 Meeting House Rd., 518-456-7890
home.shakerheritage.org

ENGAGE WITH LITERARY MASTERS
AT THE NYS WRITERS INSTITUTE

Serving as a nerve center for wordsmiths and literature enthusiasts, the New York State Writers Institute hosts an array of events that spotlight the world's literary luminaries and up-and-coming talents. Attend the Visiting Writers Series, which features readings, Q&As, and book signings with authors from various genres. If you're an aspiring writer, you'll want to attend the institute's writing workshops led by accomplished authors. The institute also presents a grand event, the Albany Book Festival, hosting a fantastic mix of authors and vendors annually. Biannually, the book festival announces the New York State Author and the New York State Poet. Every occasion at the NYS Writers Institute is an opportunity to explore new perspectives, meet like-minded literature enthusiasts, and get your favorite book signed by its author.

University at Albany, 1400 Washington Ave., 518-442-5620
nyswritersinstitute.org

TIP
Look for the Albany Film Festival hosted at the University of Albany in the spring. Showing feature films, as well as short film screenings, authors and filmmakers are invited to participate in panel discussions.

CLIMB THE MILLION DOLLAR STAIRCASE
AT THE NEW YORK STATE CAPITOL

Unfold layers of history and architectural splendor by touring the New York State Capitol, a National Historic Landmark. This magnificent building boasts a mix of architectural styles, including Italian Renaissance and Romanesque. Within its hallowed halls, you can explore the Senate Chamber, famed for its elaborate gaslit chandeliers and richly colored ceiling, or the Assembly Chamber, filled with ornate woodwork and stately portraits. Take advantage of the awe-inspiring Great Western Staircase, often called the Million Dollar Staircase, adorned with carvings of historical and mythical figures and a marvel of craftsmanship with its 444 steps. Experience the rich past of the state firsthand through free guided tours. Learn about Theodore Roosevelt's fitness routine of running up and down the capitol's 77 front steps. Here's an interesting tidbit: the New York State Capitol was the most expensive government building of its time, costing over $25 million! The building was so costly that it was the first significant US public building to be paid for entirely by its citizens' taxes.

State St. and Washington Ave., 518-474-2418
ogs.ny.gov/location/new-york-state-capitol

TIP

Free capitol tours are available three times a day, Monday through Friday. But in October, tours take on a ghastly turn. The Capitol Hauntings Tour revisits the time when a night watchman died in a fire and the legend of the Secret Demon was born. Guests also hear which two US presidents visited after their deaths and the tale of the tortured artist who painted the Assembly Chamber's hidden murals.

empirestateplaza.ny.gov/tours/
new-york-state-capitol

TOUR THE FUTURISTIC ART AND ARCHITECTURE
AT THE EMPIRE STATE PLAZA

Explore a mesmerizing fusion of contemporary art and monumental architecture at Empire Plaza. The 98-acre plaza features an array of government skyscrapers, monuments, and a rich collection of modern art, making it an essential stop for architecture and art buffs. The site is home to the formidable Corning Tower, New York State's tallest building outside of NYC. Take advantage of free admission to the tower's 42nd-floor observatory; it offers panoramic views of Albany and beyond, from the Hudson River Valley to the Adirondack Mountains. Outdoors, the plaza is dotted with artworks from internationally acclaimed artists such as Alexander Calder, Ellsworth Kelly, and Louise Nevelson. Calder's monumental black *Triangles and Arches* contrasts beautifully with George Sugarman's canary-hued *Trio*, adding vibrancy to the plaza's stark Brutalist backdrop. Underground, look for paintings by Jackson Pollock, Mark Rothko, and Helen Frankenthaler. Described by art historians as "the greatest collection of modern American art in any single public site that is not a museum," this is an Albany must-do.

Empire State Plaza, 100 S Mall Arterial, 518-474-2418
empirestateplaza.ny.gov

TIP

Learn about the buildings that make up the
Empire State Plaza on a free walking tour,
available July through August. Or head out on
the Trolley Tour, which covers additional local
landmarks, art, memorials, and history. It also
runs through the summer.

empirestateplaza.ny.gov

FOLLOW THE CLUES
IN THE CHERRY HILL MURDER MYSTERY

Dig into an engaging slice of history at Historic Cherry Hill, a 1787 Georgian mansion. Here, you'll find yourself enveloped in the infamous 1827 Cherry Hill murder, a crime that shook Albany society. The mansion's tour isn't just about elegant architecture and historical artifacts; it's an investigative journey into one of Albany's most captivating historical mysteries. The guided Murder Mystery tour takes you through the saga of the ill-fated lovers, the wealthy tenant farmer, and the violent confrontation that led to one of the last hangings in Albany. You'll explore rooms frozen in time, where echoes of passion, betrayal, and retribution still linger. Each year, the mansion hosts a dramatic retelling of the murder, bringing this tragic story alive. At Cherry Hill, you don't just learn about history—you experience it firsthand, diving into the intrigue and drama of Albany's past.

523½ S Pearl St., 518-434-4791
historiccherryhill.org

CONNECT WITH ARTISTS
AT THE ALBANY CENTER GALLERY

Immerse yourself in a world of local artistry at the Albany Center Gallery. The gallery spotlights the region's incredible talent with a mission to bring the power of visual art to the forefront of community life. The wide array of exhibits rotating throughout the year allows you to explore a kaleidoscope of mediums, styles, and themes, from cutting-edge contemporary art to traditional landscape painting. Its collection changes frequently, continually offering new perspectives to visitors. Along with a display space, the gallery actively champions local artists, providing a platform to showcase their work and interact with art lovers. It also hosts engaging workshops, artist talks, and networking events, making it a thriving hub for artists and art enthusiasts. Visiting here will fill your day with evocative images and give you an intimate view of the region's lively art scene.

488 Broadway, #107, 518-462-4775
albanycentergallery.org

ANOTHER GALLERY

The Opalka Gallery, located on the Sage College of Albany campus, showcases contemporary and modern art in the region. Featuring renowned artists and emerging talents, the gallery provides a platform for innovative visual arts, lectures, and public programs.

140 New Scotland Ave., 518-292-7742
opalka.sage.edu

NURTURE ART AND COMMUNITY
AT THE ALBANY BARN

Rooted in neighborhood spirit, the Albany Barn blossomed from Rock2Rebuild™, a grassroots group whose fundraising events benefited local artists and worthy causes. Now the 13,000-square-foot arts incubator operates from the former St. Joseph's Academy schoolhouse in an Arbor Hill district, continuing its mission to build community while fostering local artists. The space provides 22 low-cost, live-work residencies for artists while hosting eclectic programming across artistic disciplines. This programming can include, but is not limited to, art exhibits, painting classes, rehearsal space, a songwriters' circle, and African drum and dance classes. By championing local talent and partnering with local groups, Albany Barn helps ensure that art, in its myriad forms, remains front and center in the Capital District.

56 2nd St., 518-935-4858
albanybarn.org

TIP

The Albany Barn collaborates with the Albany Center Gallery on Capital Walls, a public art project that brings living color murals to Downtown Albany. Check out the illustrated tour map on the website for a self-guided tour or sign up for upcoming walking and bike tours.
albanycentergallery.org/capitalwalls

VENTURE ABOARD
THE HISTORIC USS *SLATER*

Step into history aboard the USS *Slater*, the last remaining World War II–era Cannon-class destroyer escort in the US. Initially launched in 1944, the *Slater* served with distinction in both the Atlantic and Pacific theaters. After the war, she was transferred to the Greek Navy but was later returned to the US in the 1990s for restoration. Today, docked on the Hudson River, she tells her tale to all who tread her decks. Expert guides lead you through her meticulously restored spaces, from the ominous torpedo tubes and powerful deck guns to the crew's cramped quarters and austere galley. Relive history in the radio room where the dot-dash rhythm of Morse code directed naval engagements, or observe the mammoth three-inch guns standing sentinel on deck. Special commemorations like Memorial Day services and a Pearl Harbor remembrance heighten the poignant resonance of this maritime treasure.

141 Broadway, 518-431-1943
ussslater.org

TRACE IRISH ROOTS
AT THE IRISH AMERICAN HERITAGE MUSEUM

The Irish American Heritage Museum is dedicated to preserving and telling the story of the contributions of the Irish people and their culture in America from the colonial era to the present day. Walk through the exhibitions and learn about the Great Hunger, the impact of Irish Americans on the building of America, and their contributions to music, literature, sports, and politics. Interactive displays bring to life this vibrant immigrant community's struggles, triumphs, and enduring influence. Take part in regular events like traditional Irish music nights, lectures, and book launches, which will further enrich your understanding. The Irish American Heritage Museum doesn't just recount history; it lets you live a part of it. Whether you have Irish roots or are interested in history, this museum will provide a compelling visit.

21 Quackenbush Sq., 518-427-1916
irish-us.org

SPARK CREATIVITY
AT THE ARTS CENTER
OF THE CAPITAL REGION

Unleash your artistic side at the Arts Center of the Capital Region. This dynamic hub is not just a gallery; it's a creative incubator, offering over 800 classes annually in everything from painting and pottery to dance and digital art. Inside the center's historic 36,000-square-foot building, 11 state-of-the-art studios buzz with the energy of creatives honing their crafts. Walk the galleries and marvel at the rotating exhibitions of local and national artists, sure to inspire and provoke thought. Perhaps you'll be drawn to the black box theater, home to intriguing performances, or tempted to sign up for a one-off workshop to explore a new medium. Make sure to attend their signature events like the annual Fence Show, exhibiting works by member artists; the name references the days when artwork was displayed on an iron fence around Troy's Washington Park. At the Arts Center of the Capital Region, it's your turn to embrace creativity and artistic exploration.

265 River St., Troy, 518-273-0552
artscenteronline.org

UNCOVER THE STORY OF "YANKEE DOODLE"
AT CRAILO STATE HISTORIC SITE

Return to the 1600s at Crailo State Historic Site and get a fascinating insight into the Dutch colonial period of the Hudson River Valley. This historic site, originally part of the vast Van Rensselaer family patroonship, includes a striking, early 18th-century brick manor house named Crailo, after the family's ancestral estate in the Netherlands. Inside, the detailed exhibits offer a fascinating look into the lives of the Dutch settlers, from their daily routines and culture to their interactions with Native American communities. Among the significant artifacts is a collection of archaeological treasures from the Fort Orange excavation. A true historical gem, Crailo is also believed to be the birthplace of the famous song "Yankee Doodle." It's said that during the French and Indian War, a British surgeon stationed here wrote the initial verses of the song as a way to mock colonial troops. Crossing the threshold of Crailo State Historic Site, you'll walk through centuries of history and trace the roots of a quintessential American tune.

9½ Riverside Ave., Rensselaer, 518-463-8738
parks.ny.gov/historic-sites/crailo/details.aspx

WALK THROUGH PRESIDENTIAL HISTORY
AT THE MARTIN VAN BUREN NATIONAL HISTORIC SITE

The Martin Van Buren National Historic Site, also known as Lindenwald, was the 19th-century home of America's eighth president. Today, this rural estate affords a unique glimpse into the life and career of Martin Van Buren. Guided tours take visitors through the meticulously preserved home, with its period furnishings reflecting Van Buren's refined taste. Walk through lush landscapes, including a decorative front yard and practical kitchen garden, that remain faithful to mid-1800s designs. In addition to the main house, the 125-acre site encompasses several farms and other buildings, providing an authentic reproduction of a 19th-century American farm. Throughout your visit, you'll gain insight into Van Buren's intriguing political career, from his influential role in forming the Democratic Party to his stance against the expansion of slavery, a significant era of American history. Lindenwald and the visitors center are open seasonally—generally spring through fall—but check the website to confirm. Both may also be closed if there is excessive heat as neither is air-conditioned.

1013 Old Post Rd., Kinderhook, 518-758-9689
nps.gov/mava/index.htm

WANDER AMID WORKS OF WONDER
AT ART OMI

Ramble through the extraordinary world of Art Omi, where natural landscapes meet imaginative creativity. Spread across 120 acres of the Hudson Valley, this unique sculpture and architecture park houses an array of more than 60 large-scale sculptures and architectural installations. Marvel at the whimsical *ReActor* house/sculpture, a 44-foot-long rotating home balanced on a single point, or ponder over the kinetic sound sculpture *Omi Pond House*. International artists create new installations each year, transforming the landscape into an evolving canvas. Alongside the open-air gallery and indoor exhibits at the Newmark Gallery, Art Omi also hosts residencies in visual arts, music, dance, and literature, encouraging creative interchange across cultures. A variety of educational programs and workshops inspire the next generation of artists. Art Omi offers an adventure into the fusion of art, nature, and human innovation for aspiring creatives and curious explorers that's not to be missed.

1405 Co. Rte. 22, Ghent, 518-392-4747
artomi.org

DELVE INTO VISUAL STORYTELLING
AT THE TANG TEACHING MUSEUM

Allow yourself to be intrigued by the the Frances Young Tang Teaching Museum and Art Gallery at Skidmore College, which offers creative, often boundary-blurring exhibits. This expansive 38,000-square-foot space bustles with artistic innovation. It's a fusion of academic fields, a testament to the interdisciplinary vision of its creators. Exhibitions change regularly; check the online collection for what to expect. One must-see, the Elevator Music series, turns the mundane into the extraordinary, transforming a standard elevator ride into an immersive sound-art experience. And it's a handy way to get to the rooftop where live concerts were held until their popularity forced relocation to the lawn. Additional museum events include arts and crafts, artist-led discussions, and hands-on workshops. A visit to the Tang isn't just a look into the arts but a conversation between disciplines and an exploration of critical contemporary issues.

815 N Broadway, #1632, Saratoga Springs, 518-580-8080
tang.skidmore.edu

B. Lodge & Co.

SHOPPING
AND FASHION

GIFT SWEETNESS
FROM KRAUSE'S HOMEMADE CANDY

Happiness is perusing the shelves at Krause's Homemade Candy. Established in 1929, this confectionery haven is famous for its almond buttercrunch—a treat so beloved that hundreds of pounds fly off the shelves every Christmas. Their chocolate-covered Granny Smith caramel apples also top the chart, balancing tartness, sweetness, and rich flavors in each mouthwatering bite. And who can resist a fancy high-heeled pump made entirely of scrumptious milk chocolate? Find all the most popular chocolates in the favorites box: almond buttercrunch, caramels, truffles, nut clusters, creams, peanut butter cups, cherry cordials, coconuts, and jellies. Behind the creation of these delicacies are three generations of the Krause family, their dedication to quality and tradition evident in each confection. A trip to Krause's is an indulgence in a bit of sweet, enduring heritage.

1609 Central Ave., 518-869-3950
krausescandy.com

VENTURE INTO RETAIL HERITAGE
AT B. LODGE & CO.

Get to know Albany's past and present at B. Lodge & Co. This store is a beacon of persistent success and community presence, helmed by the passionate Mark Yonally. Accepting the reins from his parents in 2011, Yonally upholds the tradition of catering to every customer with devotion and sincerity. Inside this retail time capsule, walk through a labyrinth of goods, ranging from everyday necessities to hidden gems. Every item is a testament to the store's "customer-first" mantra. Whether you're looking for hospital scrubs, socks, or designer athletic wear, the B. Lodge & Co. team ensures you find what you need. If the store doesn't have it, the friendly staff will direct you to where you can get it, upholding a generous spirit that's rare in today's retail landscape. In a world where digital giants like Amazon reign, B. Lodge & Co. stands firm as a testament to personal, local service.

75 N Pearl St., 518-463-4646
blodgeandcompany.com

PRESERVE AND ADMIRE
AT THE HISTORIC ALBANY FOUNDATION

Established in 1974, the Historic Albany Foundation has been instrumental in preserving Albany's architectural legacy. It safeguards the historical integrity of the city's structures so that future generations can appreciate Albany's rich past. Visit its Architectural Parts Warehouse, a treasure trove for anyone with a penchant for restoration. The warehouse breathes new life into old items by offering over 1,000 reclaimed doors, mantels, and stained glass windows for sale, and even a Tool Lending Library for would-be DIYers. Hear fascinating stories of local architecture by joining one of the foundation's informative walking tours led by knowledgeable guides. Whether you're an architecture aficionado, a history enthusiast, or just a curious wanderer, the Historic Albany Foundation provides an insight into Albany's past while emphasizing the significance of architectural conservation.

89 Lexington Ave., 518-465-0876
historic-albany.org

EMBRACE AN UPSTATE OF MIND
AT THE FORT ORANGE GENERAL STORE

What is an Upstate of Mind? According to Compas Life, "It's the feeling when you exhale your workweek and inhale that small-town relaxation." It makes sense that their logo gear would fly off the shelves at the Fort Orange General Store. Amble through the shop, a trove of striking home goods, gifts, and captivating curiosities. Cheeky graphic T-shirts, local prints, and colorful throw pillows are but a few of the eclectic wares on sale. Fort Orange is a crossroads where the creativity of local designers, artists, and small businesses converge. The store's name pays homage to the Dutch settlement in New Netherland, at the center of modern Albany. Situated just two blocks from the site of the original fort, the store is a testament to Albany's rich history and vibrant contemporary culture.

412 Broadway, 518-818-0105
fortorangegeneralstore.com

MAKE A LITERARY LOVE CONNECTION
AT THE BOOK HOUSE

The independent Book House of Stuyvesant Plaza, active for over 40 years, can, upon request, orchestrate a personalized literary journey. The expert staff are more like book matchmakers who can analyze your reading preferences and handpick your next read. Seek out their recommendation cards among the bookshelves—the designated "Current Favorites" often change. Venture into the adjacent Little Book House, where a treasure trove of children's literature awaits. Colorful picture books, gripping young adult novels, and ageless fairy tales populate the shelves. Let the little ones carry their picture books into the whimsical playhouse, turning reading into an interactive adventure. Frequent author events and an extensive selection of local picks draw a passionate community of bookworms. Find even more great books at the sister location, Market Street Books in Downtown Troy.

The Book House of Stuyvesant Plaza
1475 Western Ave., #62, 518-489-4761

Market Street Books
290 River St., Troy, 518-328-0045
bhny.com

SEEK JOY
AT BRAVEHEART BOOKS & BAZAAR

A lipstick-red door beckons you into a celebration of literature at Braveheart Books & Bazaar. Scotland native Louise Hendry breathed new life into the former Down in Denver Books in 2015, and Braveheart was born, named after the film whose debut coincided with her immigration to the US. This roadside house-turned-shop is a "kilt meets kitsch" reflection of Hendry's Scottish roots and houses more than books. Inside, you'll find a vibrant collection of gently used books, vintage clothes, vinyl records, and unique crafts from over 20 local vendors. Upbeat music, lollipops, and Orson, the friendly bookstore cat, add to the welcoming atmosphere. This bookstore is a hub for community activities, regularly hosting workshops, film screenings, and local events. Functioning as your personal book curator, Hendry has a knack for pairing customers with their perfect literary match.

874 NY-43, Stephentown, 518-733-6856
braveheartbooks.net

TIP
The shop closes when the mercury drops, usually from Thanksgiving through spring. Check their Instagram account for opening and closing dates.

STOCK UP ON ITALIAN STAPLES
AT CARDONA'S MARKET

Take a trip to the *Bel Paese* without leaving the Northeast at Cardona's Market, an Italian food haven that's been family-owned since 1945. Augusto and Mary Cardona's vision of bringing authentic Italian cuisine to the local community still lives on in the variety of traditional products you'll find here. The air is filled with the aroma of simmering sauces while a selection of signature sausages hangs from the ceiling. Travel with your taste buds to Tuscany with an artisanal cheese selection or create a unique antipasto platter from their spectacular range of imported olives, salami, pepperoncini, and premium balsamic vinegars. And if you're planning a picnic, their hearty subs, generously filled with high-quality ingredients, are a must-have. They also offer perfectly seasoned, ready-to-heat meals that allow you to bring the Italian home cooking experience to your kitchen.

340 Delaware Ave., 518-434-4838
cardonasmarket.com

TIP
Drop by Bella Napoli for a wide assortment of cannoli and other Italian desserts. Add in a red-checkered tablecloth and a bottle of Chianti, and you've got yourself a date-worthy meal.
672 Loudon Rd., Latham, 518-783-0196
bellanapolibakery.com

PUSH A CART
AT THE LARGEST WALMART SUPERCENTER IN THE US

When visiting Albany's Crossgates Commons, it's hard to miss the gigantic two-story Walmart, which offers a one-of-a-kind shopping experience. Covering a staggering 260,000 square feet, this supercenter dwarfs the usual Walmart Supercenters by a substantial 100,000 square feet. Designed for convenience, the ground floor houses a full-service supermarket, while the upper floor stocks many items ranging from apparel, electronics, toys, and automotive supplies to garden essentials. The store's design allows access to both floors due to its unique hillside construction. What truly sets this supercenter apart is its cart escalator, locally known as the "Cartalator." This marvel runs adjacent to the conventional escalator, transporting your shopping cart between floors. Do note that the pushcarts do not have a bottom shelf so that they can be securely attached to the Cartalator. With more room to explore and more merchandise to shop, this Walmart promises a retail adventure that will keep you coming back.

141 Washington Ave. Ext., 518-869-4694
walmart.com/store/2152-albany-ny

IGNITE CREATIVITY
AT ARLENE'S ARTIST MATERIALS

Stimulate your artistic spirit at Arlene's Artist Materials, an independent art supply store that has inspired creatives since 1960. This gold mine of art supplies is chock-full of high-quality paints, sketchbooks, brushes, and everything in between. Wander through a rainbow of colorful displays, each aisle holding a new medium awaiting experimentation. Whether you're a novice sketcher or a seasoned painter, Arlene's staff members—artists themselves—are ready to help you choose the right tools for your next masterpiece. While there, remember to check out their range of instructional books to help guide your artistic journey. With a regular rotation of in-store workshops, demonstrations, and art exhibitions, Arlene's is not just a store—it's a springboard for artists of all levels.

57 Fuller Rd., 518-482-8881
arlenesartist.com

DRESS LIKE A MILLION BUCKS
AT METROPOLIS VINTAGE

Ever dream of rocking Victorian elegance or reliving the grungy '90s? Swing on by Metropolis Vintage, and you can make that dream come true. Their collection is like a walk through time, ranging from turn-of-the-century collectibles to rad '90s pieces. Fancy wrapping yourself in luxurious fur, slipping into a classic leather jacket, or donning a 1950s ball gown accessorized with stunning costume jewelry? Metropolis has them all and so much more. And the finds? Wow! Just recently, a jaw-dropping Mary McFadden robe and a shimmering gold Jaeger jacket were on display. In business for over 40 years and offering professional estate services, Metropolis Vintage's inventory is constantly being renewed. Even better, the proprietor excels at helping customers create a look that looks good on you.

32 Fuller Rd., 518-438-8277
metropolisvintage.com

GET FITTED
AT MADAME PIRIE FAMISE CORSET SHOPPE

Old-world elegance meets modern fashion at Madame Pirie Famise Corset Shoppe. Opened on Pearl Street by Pearl Spitzer in 1945, it was one of the first woman-owned businesses in the area. Thus began a nearly 80-year history of women helping women look and feel beautiful. The key to looking good is starting with a suitable foundation garment. Here, the talented staff is renowned for expert bra fittings and finding the right undergarment for special occasions or every day. The shop specializes in bras of all sizes—from 30AA to 56O—ensuring that every woman, even a postmastectomy cancer survivor, finds her perfect fit. Top brands in intimate apparel find a home at Madame Pirie, where quality and comfort are never compromised. Whether you're seeking a sexy corset, a silky nightgown, or a T-shirt bra, you'll find your perfect fit at Madame Pirie's.

1660 Western Ave., 518-869-0400
madamepirie.com

STIR IT UP
AT CAPITAL COOKS

For decades, Different Drummer's Kitchen provided local gourmands with quality cookware, innovative gadgets, and enlightening cookbooks. They pioneered the concept of hands-on learning in the region, offering cooking classes from the early '90s until recently. But when Different Drummer's Kitchen was replaced by Sur La Table, the chefs sought a new location to host the cooking classes. Now find cooking classes, kids camps, and demonstrations at Capital Cooks. Housed in a beautiful new setting, the kitchen is state-of-the-art, with all the bells and whistles for cooking or baking anything you desire. Whether you're keen to explore exotic cuisines, learn new techniques, or are ready to master cake decorating, you'll find a class that feeds your appetite for learning.

Capital Cooks
12 Walker Way, Colonie, 518-810-8412
capitalcooksny.com

Sur La Table
1475 Western Ave. #26, 838-333-9397
stuyvesantplaza.com/surla-table

BRING FANTASY TO LIFE
AT THE COSTUMER

Bare your inner thespian, superhero, or unicorn at The Costumer, a wonderland of theatrical costumes, whimsical accessories, and dress-up supplies. This magical emporium, in business for over a century, has perfected the art of transformation. From Romeo to Rapunzel or Darth Vader to a dazzling mermaid, the costume possibilities are as limitless as your imagination. Founded over 100 years ago by Mrs. Anna White, nurtured by the Sheehan family, and now under the caring guardianship of the Johnsen clan, The Costumer continues its mission: offering unrivaled customer service with heart. Their unique blend of industry knowledge, directorial insight, and love for theater education makes every costume experience here memorable. Professionals and amateurs alike flock here for top-notch quality and variety. Whether prepping for a grand performance, gearing up for a cosplay convention, or wanting to add flair to your next party, The Costumer ensures your ensemble will be show-stopping.

Retail Store
220 Harborside Dr., Schenectady, 518-464-9031

Rental Warehouse
1020–1030 Barrett St., 518-374-7442
thecostumer.com

JOURNEY
WITH TOUGH TRAVELER

For the true adventurer, gear matters. Experience the unique blend of practicality and style at Tough Traveler, a world-renowned bag manufacturer. Established in 1970, this family-owned business has crafted innovative, durable, and ethically made products for over 50 years. Each backpack, carry-on, or luggage piece screams quality, having been crafted with meticulous attention to detail. Products are robust, built to last, and designed with a keen sense of aesthetics. Tough Traveler understands the essence of travel—comfort and reliability—and infuses it into each creation. Whether you're an urban explorer, an outdoor enthusiast, or a nomadic wanderer, Tough Traveler crafts the perfect companion for your journey. So, step inside this local factory store, and let your next adventure begin with the ideal bag in tow!

1012 State St., Schenectady, 518-377-8526
toughtraveler.com

BASK IN THE GLOW
FROM BEEKMAN 1802 KINDNESS SHOP

Enter the beguiling world of Beekman 1802 Kindness Shop, a unique retail oasis crafted by the inspiring journey of Josh Kilmer-Purcell and Dr. Brent Ridge. These two former New York City high-flyers traded skyscrapers for pastoral serenity in 2008, adopting a goat farm in Sharon Springs during the financial crisis. Their leap of faith led to the creation of the Beekman 1802 Kindness Shop and landed them on television screens nationwide with their reality TV show, *The Fabulous Beekman Boys*, which aired for two seasons and showcased their adventures in farm life. You can find their skin and body products at high-end luxury hotels as well as in this shop in the adorably quaint village of Sharon Springs.

187 Main St., Sharon Springs, 888-801-1802
beekman1802.com/pages/the-store

TIP
Make it a day-trip excursion with a hike to the summit of Vroman's Nose and a stop at the Black Cat Cafe for lunch.
visitschohariecounty.com/listing/vromans-nose
195 Main St., Sharon Springs, 518-284-2575
blackcatcafes.com

CONJURE STORIES AND MAGIC
AT AQUILONIA COMICS

Get lost in a universe of heroic tales, fantastical worlds, and vivid illustrations at Aquilonia Comics and Cards. The shop boasts a vast collection spanning the latest graphic novels, cherished classics, and a treasure trove of back issues waiting for you to recoup or complete your collection. Aquilonia Comics is also a haven for gameplay, emphasizing Magic: The Gathering. Whether you're a seasoned Planeswalker or just starting your journey, you have a seat at their tables. Join spirited matches, exchange strategies, or relish in the camaraderie of fellow enthusiasts. The store is more than just a retail space; it's a circle of old and new friends. Knowledgeable staff is ready to guide you through tales and card decks or introduce you to a plethora of collectibles. At Aquilonia Comics, a world of illustrated imagination awaits, beckoning you to embrace your inner superhero.

412 Fulton St., Troy, 518-271-1069
aquiloniacomicsandcards.com

BROWSE THE BOUTIQUES
OF STUYVESANT PLAZA

Meet with friends at Stuyvesant Plaza, where boutique shopping and tempting dining converge. Kick off at Circles, for high-end fashion, luxury cosmetics, and the season's freshest trends. Adventure seekers can gear up at Eastern Mountain Sports, and for the young (or young at heart), G. Willikers offers an enchanting toy haven. Meanwhile, Pearl Grant Richmans tempts with its exquisite selection of gifts and gourmet treasures. Hungry? Peaches Café delivers on the promise of mouthwatering Belgian waffles and savory sandwiches. As for dinner or a drink, Josie's Table stands out with its farm-to-table dishes and a bar renowned for natural wines and handcrafted cocktails. Seasonal flowers and inviting benches adorn the outdoor plaza, making for a pleasant spot for a leisurely stroll, whether between shops or after a rich meal.

1475 Western Ave., 518-813-4959
stuyvesantplaza.com

GRAZE ON TASTY TREATS
AT TROY WATERFRONT
FARMERS MARKET

The place to meet on summer Saturdays is at the Troy Waterfront Farmers Market. Running continuously for over 20 years, with winters indoors at the Uncle Sam Atrium, the farmers market has grown. These days, it completely takes over Downtown Troy, weaving around Monument Square and into local streets. Most businesses embrace the market, adding tents and special treats on display in front of their shops. It's enormous, with over 80 vendors offering fresh local produce, artisanal foods, handcrafted goods, and craft beverages. Learn about sustainable farming from passionate cultivators like Denison Farm and Windy Hill Goat Dairy. Relish scrumptious sourdough from Placid Baker, and let R&G Cheese Makers—praised by the *New York Times*—introduce you to their savory selection. From Argyle Brewing Company's craft beers to Harvest Spirits' applejack, there are libations for every palate. Taste free samples, hear their stories, and perhaps take home a bottle or two.

Monument Sq., Troy, 518-708-4216
troymarket.org

STROLL DOWN LARK STREET:
BOHEMIAN VIBES & UNIQUE FINDS

Lark Street is like New York City's Greenwich Village on a funkier scale. A mosaic of 19th-century brownstones and vivid murals set the stage, each telling tales of the city's spirited arts culture. Dive into the unique boutiques that line the street: Alacrity Frame Workshop & Art Gallery showcases local artists, while Elissa Halloran Designs features crafted jewelry and vintage wares. Seasons Skate Shop carries all the hardware, clothing, and accessories boarders require. Craving something distinct? Yamaguchie offers custom woodwork and quirky chenille objects d'art. Cafés beckon with the aroma of freshly brewed coffee, the perfect backdrop for people-watching and daydreaming. As evening approaches, the air fills with jazzy rhythms and contemporary beats from local performance venues. Dining options are global—from Thai delicacies to innovative vegan dishes. Venturing down Lark Street plunges you into a curious world of craft and culture.

larkstreetbid.org

TIP

From June to October, Albany Twilight Market hosts a Vintage Night Market for strange and unusual wares at Trinity Church, which may include anything from taxidermy to curated antiques. Vendors, tarot readers, and vegan food are also present. In December, the market moves to the Washington Park Lakehouse.

albanytwilightmarket.com

HUNT FOR TREASURES
ON WARREN STREET

If you haven't returned to Warren Street in recent years, you're in for a pleasant surprise. Once practically a ghost town, Hudson's Warren Street buzzes with energy these days. The mile-long portion of the street that extends from Promenade Hill Park on the Hudson River to the Rivertown Lodge Tavern now sports a Brooklyn vibe (perhaps because, until recently, it housed an Etsy satellite office) but with easy parking. If you appreciate silver plates or the ornate, the antique shops will be right up your alley. For art aficionados, the galleries are must-visits. And for those with a keen eye for design, the mid-century modern shops (there's more than one) offer a curated selection of timeless pieces that add a touch of sophistication to any space. And when hunger pangs hit, Warren Street doesn't disappoint. From upscale bistros to quaint eateries, there's a flavor for every foodie.

Promenade Hill Park
2 Warren St., Hudson

731 Warren St., Hudson, 518-512-0954
rivertownlodge.com

ACTIVITIES
BY SEASON

• •

FALL

Satisfy Your Sweet Tooth at Cider Belly Doughnuts, 8

Dine with Ghosts at The Olde English Pub & Pantry, 7

Hoist a Telephone Pole at the Capital District Scottish Games, 42

Climb the Million Dollar Staircase at the New York State Capitol, 98

Find Famous Americans at the Albany Rural Cemetery, 93

Bring Fantasy to Life at The Costumer, 126

Leaf Peep under a Waterfall at Thacher Park, 67

WINTER

Glide across the Empire State Plaza Ice Rink, 60

Slide into Action at the Albany Curling Club, 69

Glimmer with Giving at Capital Holiday Lights, 50

Gift Sweetness from Krause's Homemade Candy, 114

Stride through Snowy Trails at Five Rivers, 80

Conquer Winter at Maple Ski Ridge, 68

NYS Museum carousel

SUGGESTED
ITINERARIES

EMPIRE STATE PLAZA

HISTORY SEEKERS

ART LOVERS

• •

MUSIC LOVERS

OUTDOOR ADVENTURERS

• •

FAMILY FUN

Conquer Winter at Maple Ski Ridge, 68

Ride the Zipper at the Altamont Fair, 39

Spin Back Time at Guptill's Roller-Skating Arena, 51

Explore Epochs at the New York State Museum, 94

Enjoy Vintage Rides at Huck Finn's Playland, 47

Revel in the Grandeur of the Palace Theatre, 40

Glimmer with Giving at Capital Holiday Lights, 50

ROMANCE

Glide across the Empire State Plaza Ice Rink, 60

Graze on Tasty Treats at Troy Waterfront Farmers Market, 131

Charm Your Sweetheart at the Iron Gate Cafe, 3

Splurge at Yono's for a Big Night Out, 26

Hunt for Treasures on Warren Street, 134

Indulge in Spirited Ice Cream at Boozy Moo!, 28

WORTH THE DRIVE

Race the Fast and Furious at Lebanon Valley Speedway, 57

Journey to the Center of the Earth at Howe Caverns, 84

Hedge Your Bets at the Saratoga Race Course, 56

Mangia in Schenectady's Little Italy, 30

Step Up to Bat at the Baseball Hall of Fame, 83

• •

Little *Nipper*

INDEX

● ●

• •